SECOND EDITION

STUDY
listening

A course in listening to lectures and note-taking

Tony Lynch

For Mauricéa

CAMBRIDGE UNIVERSITY PRESS
Cambridge, New York, Melbourne, Madrid, Cape Town,
Singapore, São Paulo, Delhi, Tokyo, Mexico City

Cambridge University Press
The Edinburgh Building, Cambridge CB2 8RU, UK

www.cambridge.org
Information on this title: www.cambridge.org/9780521533874

First published 2004
7th printing 2011

Printed in the United Kingdom at the University Press, Cambridge

A catalogue record for this publication is available from the British Library

ISBN 978-0-521-53387-4 Paperback
ISBN 978-0-521-54858-8 Audio CD Set (2)
ISBN 978-0-521-54857-1 Audio Cassette Set (2)

Cambridge University Press has no responsibility for the persistence or
accuracy of URLs for external or third-party internet websites referred to in
this publication, and does not guarantee that any content on such websites is,
or will remain, accurate or appropriate. Information regarding prices, travel
timetables and other factual information given in this work is correct at
the time of first printing but Cambridge University Press does not guarantee
the accuracy of such information thereafter.

The authors and publishers are grateful for permission to use the copyright materials
appearing in this book, as indicated in the sources and acknowledgements throughout.
If there are errors or omissions the publishers would be pleased to hear and to make
the appropriate correction in future reprints.

Contents

Acknowledgements

I would like to thank all the people who helped me to produce this new edition of *Study Listening*: the eight featured speakers – Adrienne Hunter, Olwyn Alexander, Ron Howard, Hugh Trappes-Lomax, Eric Glendinning, Harry Griffin, Mauricéa Lynch and Simon Allen; Alan Whyte, who supervised the recordings; the teachers in various countries who tried out and commented on the pilot materials – and in particular Kathy Cox and David Hill in Sydney, who provided detailed and helpful feedback on the complete draft; my Institute for Applied Language Studies colleagues Cathy Benson, Anne Heller-Murphy and Michael Jenkins for letting me intrude on their listening processes; the Cambridge University Press staff involved in the editing – Linda Matthews, Will Capel and Mickey Bonin; and Hart McLeod for design and layout. Last but not least, I would like to express my thanks to the EAP and ELTT students at the Institute for Applied Language Studies of the University of Edinburgh, who have worked with me on several generations of classroom listening materials over the 20 years since the first edition came out.

To the Student

Who is the book for?

Study Listening is for adult learners of English who are planning to study at a university or college where English is the language of instruction, or who need to attend international conferences where English is used.

To make the most effective use of *Study Listening* your overall English level needs to be at least 5.0 IELTS, 500 TOEFL or 173 CBT-TOEFL.

What do we listen to?

Study Listening has been written for people from a range of academic fields. Have a look at the *Course Map* (page 9) to see which topics are covered in the course. You should find the content of the eight main lectures accessible to you, even if you are not a specialist in that subject.

The speakers you will be listening to come from six different countries. This will help you to get used to some of the international accents of English, including English as a second language.

How do we improve our listening?

According to the proverb, 'Practice makes perfect' – but a lot depends on what sort of practice you get. In *Study Listening* you will be working through three stages of classroom activity to help you increase your ability to understand and take notes on lectures – before, while and after listening.

Before listening to each lecture you will be discussing the content and language that you can expect the lecturer to use. When we hear lectures as part of a university course, we use our knowledge of the subject to help us to understand what we hear. *Study Listening* simulates that real-life situation through pre-listening discussion, which helps you to call up the background knowledge and relevant language in preparation for what the lecturer says.

While listening to the lectures you will be practising the skills you need to make notes. Combining listening and writing in this way is not easy, even in our first language, so this book highlights techniques for making your notes shorter but effective.

After-listening tasks are of two kinds. First, there are tasks in which you analyse the *language* used by the lecturer, for example listening in detail to parts of the talk where the lecturer spoke quickly or used an unusual expression. Second, there are tasks that focus on the *content* of the lecture. Here you get a chance to express your views on the lecture topic, to argue against the points the speaker made, to extend the discussion beyond what was said in the lecture, and so on.

A new feature of *Study Listening* is the activity called *Troubleshooting*. This is intended to help your teacher to focus on the particular problems that students in your class have had as you took notes on the lecture. Exactly what your teacher will concentrate on depends on what your particular problems were. In each unit, I give you an example of a difficulty that my students in Edinburgh have needed to work on to overcome.

Listening practice for IELTS

Study Listening is not simply a preparation for a university language test such as IELTS (International English Language Testing System). The listening, note-taking and troubleshooting tasks in *Study Listening* are designed to help you cope with the longer passages of listening that you will encounter in university lectures. However, most of the units in *Study Listening* include tasks that are similar to those in the IELTS Listening module, such as completing a note-frame, filling in gaps in a text and identifying main points. Other tasks are designed to resemble those in the IELTS Speaking and Writing modules. All these tasks have been marked with an IELTS symbol.

For practice specifically targeted at the shorter listening passages in IELTS, I would recommend *Insight into IELTS* by Jakeman and McDowell (Cambridge University Press).

I hope very much that you will enjoy using *Study Listening* and that you will find it helps you to listen to English more effectively and confidently. If you would like to tell me about your experience of using the book, you are very welcome to email me at A.J.Lynch@ed.ac.uk

Tony Lynch
Edinburgh
Scotland

To the Teacher Changes from the first edition

If you used the original edition of *Study Listening*, you will find this new edition very different, reflecting the developments in the teaching of listening in recent years.

Thematic structure

The new edition begins with an Introduction unit on note-taking techniques. Units 1–8 each feature a lecture on an academic topic, then the course is rounded off by a *Final review* offering strategic advice. The lectures increase in length from 7 to 23 minutes.

Macrostrategies

A second departure from the first edition is the presentation and practice of six general cognitive and metacognitive Macrostrategies. These macrostrategies are based on the findings of recent research into foreign language listening (for example, Vandergrift 1999, Rost 2002) and comprise Predicting, Monitoring, Responding, Clarifying, Inferencing and Evaluating. They are introduced in Unit 1, then each is practised separately in Units 2 to 6. They are then reviewed and integrated through work on the lectures in Units 7 and 8.

Post-listening activities

There is a greater role for post-listening work, which was limited in the first edition to discussion of the content of the talk. In this second edition, I have built on recent proposals (such as those of Field 1998, White 1998) for an expansion of the post-listening phase to include analysis of spoken language and speaker delivery. In particular, I have adopted the notion of 'troubleshooting' (Tauroza 1995), in which the teacher and students work together in analysing what has caused their comprehension problems, so that the teacher can provide appropriate practice activities.

Transcript listening

In the first edition, the lecture transcripts were used mainly to check answers. For the past few years I have been using transcripts as a means of improving students' listening. I should emphasise, though, that the transcript is used only *after* the class has already completed two cycles of listening and note-taking. The transcripts are used as a tool for helping students to 'focus on form', including the particular forms created naturally in rapid speech.

A typical unit

Pre-listening
> Notes on a macrostrategy
> Introductory reading text
> Brainstorming ideas about lecture content
> Focal points of vocabulary or grammar

First listening
> Guided note-taking for main ideas and development
> Focus on relevant macrostrategy
> Oral summary

Second listening
> Detailed note-taking
> Comparison of notes – content and form

After listening
> *Focus on language*
>> Troubleshooting (analysis of listening problems, such as speed and accent)
>> Marking-up tasks using transcript (for example for stress, pausing, rapid speech)
>> Focus on form (such as markers of argument and importance)
>
> *Focus on content*
>> Clarifying
>> Critical thinking
>> Personal response tasks
>> Optional follow-up (for example, writing a short essay)

Materials

The total length of the recordings is just under 2 hours and they are available on either two CDs or two C60 audiocassettes.

You will find *Teaching notes* for each unit at the back of the book, with suggestions for handling the materials and tasks, and a short *Appendix* containing materials on academic vocabulary.

Timing

The book provides teaching materials for 25–30 hours' classroom work, depending on the level and pace of the group. I estimate the class time as follows: Introduction (60–90 minutes), Units 1–8 (2½–3 hours each) and Final Review (60–90 minutes). There is also some variation within Units 1–8, as the earlier lectures are shorter than the later ones.

Course Map

Topic	Macro focus on strategies	Micro focus on language/skills (some examples)
Introduction 'Two functions of listening'	Note-taking techniques	Listening problems in lectures Spoken and written English
Unit 1 'Problems of urbanisation'	Macrostrategy 1: Predicting	Signpost and list markers Hedging
Unit 2 'Differences between academic cultures'	Macrostrategy 2: Monitoring	Quotations and direct speech Different meanings of 'or' Markers of conclusion Critical thinking
Unit 3 'Teleworking and distance learning'	Macrostrategy 3: Responding	Importance markers Definitions and explanations Coping with fast speech
Unit 4 'Language strategies for awkward situations'	Macrostrategy 4: Clarifying	Expressions of contrast Exploiting a handout Politeness strategies
Unit 5 'Targets for preventive medicine'	Macrostrategy 5: Inferencing	Recognising word stress Coping with fast speech Exploiting 'recycling' of information
Unit 6 'Cloning: The significance of Dolly'	Macrostrategy 6: Evaluating	Using reading input Identifying negative and positive arguments Recognising word stress
Unit 7 'Measuring quality of life'	Integrating Macrostrategies 1–6	Listening to a non-native accent Using a PowerPoint handout Identifying chains of meaning
Unit 8 'Climate change: Evidence and action'	Integrating Macrostrategies 1–6	Noticing changes of topic Recognising speaker attitude Distinguishing actual from potential events
Final review 'Ways of continuing to improve your listening'	Listening practice strategies	Types and sources of listening Critiquing advice on listening Assessing listening needs

INTRODUCTION
Two functions of listening

This unit aims to develop listening skills by:

1. sharing experiences of lectures as orientation to the topic
2. identifying the listening problems in lectures
3. discussing the differences between spoken and written English
4. discussing different note-taking techniques
5. introducing the Macrostrategies for listening.

Defining a lecture

There are different types of lecture. In a university setting, a lecture is normally one of a series given by the same lecturer as part of a degree course. The lecturer usually talks for 45–60 minutes, and longer in some cultures. The students listen, make notes and may ask questions.

The purpose of a lecture may be the presentation and understanding of facts and ideas, rather than an exchange between lecturer and students. (A university class where the emphasis is on interaction and discussion of ideas is usually called a *seminar* or *tutorial*.)

Your experience of lectures

Share your experiences of lectures by considering and discussing your responses to the following questions.
1 Have you attended other types of lecture? Where?
2 Were they given in your own language or in English (or both)?
3 Did you need to take notes?
4 Have you ever given lectures yourself?

Lecturing styles
Lecturing styles vary from place to place, and even from person to person in the same place. But it has been said that in general there are three main types:
- reading style
- conversational style
- rhetorical style.

In the *reading* style, the lecturer either reads aloud from a script or speaks as if they were reading it.

In the *conversational* – or *interactive* – style, the lecturer speaks from brief notes, using relatively informal language, and probably encourages the students to contribute by asking questions or responding to points in the lecture.

The *rhetorical* style is rather like a performance in the theatre; the lecture includes not just the presentation of facts but also stories, jokes and digressions. (In many universities in Britain – and perhaps in other countries – a lecture room is also called a *lecture theatre*.)

1 In your country, do you find all three styles of lecture?
2 What do you think are the advantages of each of the styles?
3 Is one of the styles easier to understand than the others?

Difficulties in lectures

1 Have you ever had difficulty listening to lectures in your own language?
2 List the things that might make it difficult to *hear* or *understand* what a lecturer is saying. Use the four headings below.
   a) Physical setting

   b) Speaker

   c) Subject

   d) Language

Effective lecturing

What speaking techniques and lecturing technology can lecturers use to help students understand what they are saying?

Spoken and written language

1 What are the main differences between speech and writing?
2 Most international students find that listening to a lecture in

English is more difficult than reading the same information. Very few think that reading is harder than listening. What is your view? What makes one activity easier for you than the other?

Listening

TASK 1 1 Your teacher is going to play you the first minute of a short talk by Tony Lynch, about two functions of listening. Listen carefully. Which do you think he is doing:
a) reading a script
b) speaking from notes
c) speaking without notes?

2 Do you think that the way he speaks shows any of the features you discussed under points 1 and 2 of *Spoken and written language* (above)?

Note-taking in lectures

For many of us, what makes listening to lectures difficult – and tiring – is having to listen and write notes at the same time.
The listener has to decide the following.

Step 1   What is being said.

Step 2   What it means (how it relates to what has been said).

Step 3   Whether it is important and whether to note it down.

Step 4   How to write it in note form.

In that decision-making process, the most important part is step 3 – evaluating the importance of information. Notice that it depends on our *knowledge of the subject*, rather than our knowledge of English.

Note-taking techniques

TASK 2 Consider your responses to the following questions.
1 How is note-taking different from dictation?
2 What is the purpose of making notes?
3 Who are notes written for?

Note-taking is a very personal thing and there is no single best system. But there are three basic rules that help to make note-taking quicker and more efficient.

Rule 1   **Be selective:** decide what's important.

Rule 2   **Be brief:** use abbreviations and symbols.

Rule 3   **Be clear:** show the interrelationship between the speaker's points.

Rule 1: Be selective

Imagine that a first-year undergraduate and a first-year postgraduate studying the same subject have attended the same lecture. In what ways do you think their notes would differ?

Rule 2: Be brief

1 What do these conventional abbreviations (of Latin origin) mean?
    a) e.g.

    b) N.B.

    c) i.e.

    d) etc.

    e) cf.

    f) v.v.

2 What do the initials below stand for? Which others are common in your academic subject?
    a) ILO

    b) WHO

    c) OPEC

    d) ABC

    e) UNESCO

3 As well as using 'official' abbreviations, you can of course invent your own. Below are some that you will find in the sample notes in this book. What *could* you use them to mean in your field?
    a) imp   b) bt

    c) int'l   d) ess'l

    e) fut   f) est

    g) prob   h) S

4 Symbols are a powerful tool in note-taking, enabling us to express complex ideas in a time-efficient way. Write in a symbol alongside each of the meanings below, and vice versa.

	Symbol	Meaning
a)		'is the same as'
b)	+	
c)		'causes' or 'leads to' or 'results in'
d)	??	
e)		'is greater than'
f)	!	
g)		'grows', 'rises', or 'raises'
h)	←	
i)		'varies with' or 'changes according to'

Rule 3: Be clear

The relationships between the ideas in a lecture are important, and notes need to reflect them – for example, chains of cause and effect. There are two common ways of representing these relationships: traditional *linear notes* and the alternative *mind map* (sometimes also called *spider notes* or *web notes*).

Below are two examples of the same information, in those two formats.

Linear notes

Spoken English
- Speak in short 'chunks'
- Simpler grammar - more coordination
- hesitations, slips
- varying accents

Written Eng.
- longer sentences
- more subordination
- text edited, 'polished'
- single standard variety

Mind map

Do you make notes in one of those two styles, or a different one?

LISTENING

Listening and note-taking

IELTS **TASK 3** We are now going to hear the whole of Tony Lynch's short talk on the 'Two functions of listening'. It practises both listening for the relationship between the points a lecturer wants to make, and also making notes that make that relationship clear. Decide first whether you want to make *linear notes* or a *mind map* – or some other style of notes.

You will hear the talk played once without stopping. It takes less than 4 minutes.

As you listen, **make notes** on the main points. Concentrate on making clear how the points relate to each other.

Comparing notes

After hearing the talk, compare the *content* of your notes with those of another student. Ask yourselves the following:
a) Have you included the same information?
b) If you missed any points, has your partner made notes on them?
c) If there were points (or words or sections) that neither of you could understand, can others in the class help?

Now compare the *form* of your notes. For this you will need to put them side-by-side. Look for differences between the ways in which you have used:
- abbreviations
- symbols
- spatial layout (for example linear notes or spider's web)
- emphasis (such as underlining and capital letters).

If you want to compare your notes with those of a native speaker, you will find a sample set of notes on the talk in *Transcripts and sample notes* on page 133.

Strategies for listening

So far in this introductory unit we have looked at detailed note-taking techniques at the micro-level which can help to make note-making quicker. But researchers have also found that people who are successful in listening to a foreign language tend to use a number of broad general strategies – which we will call *Macrostrategies* – to help themselves before, during and after listening.

MACROSTRATEGIES

1 **Predicting** Thinking about the possible content of the lecture before you listen
2 **Monitoring** Noticing your problems as you listen and identifying areas of uncertainty
3 **Responding** Giving your own opinion on the ideas presented by the lecturer
4 **Clarifying** Preparing questions that you can ask the lecturer so as to get a clearer understanding
5 **Inferencing** Making hypotheses when you aren't sure of something, such as the meaning of an unfamiliar word or expression
6 **Evaluating** Assessing how well you have understood the lecture.

During this course we will first focus on each of these macrostrategies separately (in Units 1–6), then use them in combination (Units 7 and 8).

UNIT 1 Problems of urbanisation

This unit aims to develop listening skills by:

1 introducing Macrostrategy 1, Predicting
2 showing how to make use of signpost and list markers when listening
3 providing practice in note-taking
4 explaining aspects of hedging.

MACROSTRATEGY 1 PREDICTING

We make predictions all the time. For example, we predict how long it will take to write an email, or how a friend will react to some news we have to give them, or what will be in the morning's newspaper headlines.

When listening to a foreign language we can use two main types of information to help us to predict what is going to be said next.

Background knowledge
• general knowledge of the world
• knowledge of the foreign culture
• specific subject knowledge

Context
• the situation (who is speaking, where and when)
• the co-text – what has been said so far

Guessing ahead in this way is particularly relevant in lectures. You can use your subject knowledge to help you predict what the lecturer is likely to say. In this unit you will be using what you know, and what you read in a short text, to help predict what might be included in a lecture on urban problems.

PRE-LISTENING
Introduction to the lecture topic: Urbanisation

Consider your answers to the following.
1 Do people in your country generally prefer to live in the countryside or the city?
2 Do you think this is the same in other countries – especially in developing countries?

In this unit we consider:
• the reasons that drive people to move from the country to the city
• the effects of that on the process of urbanisation
• possible policies to reduce rural–urban migration.

Concern over the differences between rural and urban life is not new. More than 30 years ago the economist and ecologist E.F. Schumacher described some of the problems in a paper entitled 'Two million villages'.

Reading

TASK 1 1 Read the text and underline the sentence that you think best summarises Schumacher's argument.

Why is it so difficult for the rich to help the poor? One of the greatest problems in the modern world is the imbalance between city and countryside in terms of wealth, power, culture, and hope. The city attracts people while the countryside does not. However, just as a sound mind depends on a sound body, so the health of the cities depends on the health of the rural areas. The cities, despite all their wealth, are simply secondary producers; primary production, the precondition of all economic life, takes place in the countryside.

To restore a proper balance between city and rural life is perhaps the greatest task facing modern societies. It is not simply a matter of raising agricultural production so as to avoid world hunger. There is no answer to the evils of mass unemployment and mass migration into cities, unless the whole level of rural life can be raised. This requires the development of an agro-industrial culture, so that each district, each community, can offer a rich variety of occupations to its members.

(adapted from Schumacher 1973: 170–171)

2 Show a partner the sentence you have underlined. Have you chosen the same one?

3 Why do you think Schumacher chose the title 'Two million villages'?

Pre-listening discussion: Content

1 Cities in developing countries grow much faster than those elsewhere. Why do you think that is?

2 What are the positive changes to the environment of a place as it becomes urbanised?

3 The title of the lecture includes the word *problems*. What problems do you predict the speaker will mention?

4 What do you expect the speaker to talk about, apart from the problems themselves?

Pre-listening discussion: Language

Here are six key expressions selected from the lecture:

infrastructure   *growth rate*   *productivity*
congestion   *depopulation*   *endemic*

Discuss their meanings with another student. If you need to, check them in a dictionary or ask the teacher.

Then say what you predict the lecturer is going to say about each of the expressions, in the context of urban problems.

The lecturer

The speaker is Dr Adrienne Hunter from Toronto, Canada, who has lived and worked for many years in Cuba. As Dr Hunter gives her talk, she uses various techniques to help the listeners follow her argument. We will focus on two of them here, which you can take advantage of as you listen and make notes.

1 She uses *signpost markers* to outline the structure of her lecture.
2 She uses *list markers* to separate the points in each section of her talk.

Lecture language: Signpost markers

....
: IELTS   **TASK 2**

Signposts on roads show the direction and distance to nearby places. In the same way, signposts in lectures are words and expressions used by the speaker to indicate the direction their talk is going to take.

At the start of the lecture you may hear signpost markers such as these:

(*what*)   *I'd like to* …   (*is*)

             I'm going to …

             I want to …

             I plan to …

             I intend to …

Then, at the start of a new section you may hear these:

so   *I'd like now to move on to* …

well   *I'd like to look now at* …

ok

all right   *turning now to* …

              moving on now to …

              having looked at X, I want to move on to …

Can you think of other expressions to add to them?

Lecture language: List markers
In the box below, the speaking sequence is left to right. What are the
missing markers?

the first			...	
	two		...	last
		thirdly	...	
first	then		...	
	another		...	

As you will hear in the lecture on urbanisation, speakers often use
list markers from different rows of the box. For example, you may
hear a lecturer say 'firstly … second … another … number four …'.

FIRST LISTENING

Listening and note-taking

TASK 3 We are now going to play the first 4 minutes of the lecture straight
through.

Make notes – but don't worry if you don't have time to note down
all the information you need to. You will get a second chance later.

As you listen, focus on the Predicting macrostrategy:

• try to predict what Adrienne Hunter is likely to say next
• use what you know and what she has said
• pay attention to the signposts and list markers in each section.

Two minutes or so from the end of the talk, the teacher will stop the
tape and ask you to predict the content of the final section.

Oral summary

TASK 4 When you have completed the first listening, work together with one
other student. Don't show each other your notes yet. Take it in turns
to use your notes to summarise the points in the sections of the
lecture.

SECOND LISTENING

Detailed note-taking

The teacher will now play the lecture a second time. Look at your notes and listen carefully for points where, during the first listening:
- you didn't catch what Adrienne Hunter said
- you didn't have time to note all the details
- you misunderstood what she said.

Comparing notes

After your second listening, put your notes next to those of another student and compare the *content* of your notes.
- Have you included the same information?
- If you missed certain points, has your partner got notes of them?

If there were points (or words or sections) that neither of you could understand, see whether others in the class can help.

Then compare the *form* of your notes. Look for differences between the ways you have used:
- abbreviations
- symbols
- layout (linear notes or spider's web, for example)
- emphasis (such as underlining and capital letters).

Then compare your notes with the sample in the *Transcripts and sample notes* section (page 135).

AFTER LISTENING

Post-listening: Focus on language

Section 1: Signpost markers

Listen to and read the first section (shown below). Underline the signpost markers.

> today I want to discuss problems of urbanisation / in particular I want to talk about those problems which are peculiar to developing economies / and to discuss three possible policies / which could be used to control or uh / to stem / uncontrolled urbanisation in
> 5 developing countries/
>
> certain urban problems of course are common to both developed / and developing countries / for example / poor housing, unemployment, problems connected with traffic / for example air pollution, congestion and so on / however there there are problems which are very peculiar

10   to developing economies / and this is due to the fact that developing
    countries need to create a basic infrastructure / which is necessary for
    industrialisation / and consequently for economic growth / in fact it's
    the provision of this infrastructure which constitutes the urbanisation
    process itself / and this uh infrastructure / or rather the / provision of
15   this infrastructure / may have undesired effects on the economy as a
    whole / now it's these undesirable consequences of ... or effects which
    I'd like to deal with first /

Section 2: List markers
Troubleshooting

IELTS

TASK 5   When they listen to the next section of the talk, some British
students find it difficult to identify all five consequences of
urbanisation. Adrienne Hunter makes clear that she had five in
mind. Identifying the first consequence and the last two is
straightforward, but the second and third consequences tend to
cause more difficulty.

1 Why should this happen? As you hear this section, **mark** the
transcript (below) with a double slash // where you think
Adrienne Hunter moved on to a new consequence.
2 Try also to **fill in** the words missing towards the end of the
section.

    I'm going to talk about five main consequences of this uncontrolled
    urbanisation / in the first instance there's the problem of the migration
20   of people from the country to the city / people living in the country
    often see the city as a more desirable place to live / whether they're
    living in developing or developed countries / but the problem is much
    more serious in a developing country / because there are / in fact
    more people who wish to migrate to the city / now the fact of people
25   migrating to the city causes a certain depopulation of rural areas /
    and a second consequence / is the result / or the result of this is a
    decrease in the production of food / and in the supply of food to the
    country as a whole / this in turn can also lead to a rise in prices /
    because of the law of supply and demand / as a result of people
30   moving to the city / you get a high urban population growth rate / now
    this isn't not this isn't due not only to the fact of more adults moving
    to the city / but can also be due to traditions of these people from
    the country / who perhaps from rural areas have a tradition of large
    families and so on / so the ci... population of the cities increases with
35   these numerous children of large families / this leads to a fourth

consequence / which is a dramatic pressure on the supply of social
services in urban areas / in particular / services related to health and
education / in relation / in relation to health services / we can see
that there are endemic diseases which could be made worse by
40 overcrowding / people coming from the country to the city / and for
example in the stresses on services in education / with more children
there's a need for more schools and more teachers and so on and so
on / a fifth area which is affected by uncontrolled urbanisation is that
of the labour supply / often uncontrolled urbanisation leads to an
45 excess of labour supply in the cities / and this can lead in turn to an
informal kind of labour activity / which might be called low-prod...
productivity activities / for example people selling things in the streets /
or for example you often find in large urban areas in a developing
country / _____ while their owners are
50 doing something else / and then they _____ when the
owners return / this is really a sort of undesirable type of labour / so
these are in fact the main consequences of uncontrolled urbanisation /

Section 3: Hedging

Hedging refers to the ways in which people express *caution* or
uncertainty about what they are saying. Adrienne Hunter used a
number of hedging expressions in the final section of her talk.

1 As you listen, read the transcript (below) and underline the words
   that show if she is certain or uncertain about whether the policies
   will be introduced and whether they will be effective.

    now I'd like to move on to three possible policies which could be
developed / to stem this kind of uncontrolled urbanisation in
55 developing countries / the first one would be to promote a more equal
land distribution / in this way farmers would be more motivated to
stay on the land / they would be able to work more land and thus be
able to feed their families more adequately / often the reason why
farmers wish to go to the city is that they cannot grow enough food
60 to both feed their families and earn a living / so a more equal land
distribution is one such policy to stem this kind of move to the city / a
second policy would be to improve the supply of social services in the
rural areas / particularly in the field of health and education / country
people often f... move to the city because they feel these services are
65 better in the city / if they could compare the services they they receive

which are improved and the ones in the city they might feel that there was perhaps not much difference / and it would be another reason for not moving / a third possible policy would be to give financial

70   assistance to agriculture / especially to the small landowner / now obviously the problem of uncontrolled urbanisation / and the consequences which are not favourable / is a difficult problem / to resolve / but these three types of policies could help to reduce the problem / which is felt in particular in developing countries/

Hedging takes various forms, and is common in both spoken and written English. Here's an example from a radio weather forecast.

Weather forecaster: *I think it's probably going to feel quite a bit cooler tomorrow, perhaps chilly even.*

The forecaster hedged by saying 'I think', 'probably' and 'perhaps'. If we take those out, we get a much more definite statement.

It's going to feel quite a bit cooler tomorrow, even chilly.

In academic English, hedging can be expressed in various ways, such as by using:
• **modal verbs** to signal degrees of certainty or commitment (*might, could, would, can, may, should, must*). It was this form of hedging that Adrienne Hunter used most in the final section of her talk
• **adjectives** (*unlikely, possible, probable*)
• **adverbs** (*perhaps, tentatively, often, usually, maybe*)
• **nouns** (*potential, uncertainty, unlikelihood*)
• the right choice of **verb** (*I suppose that …, we tend to …, this suggests that …, I would guess that …*).

Post-listening: Focus on content
Discussion and reaction
1 How did you do with your predictions? On page 18 you predicted the points you thought might be mentioned in the lecture. Did Adrienne Hunter include any of them?
2 Did she discuss any problems that are experienced in (parts of) your own country?
3 Can you think of countries where such policies have been tried out?

Critical thinking

Think of other issues relevant to the points made in Adrienne Hunter's lecture. For example, do you think that the three policies she proposed would be effective? If not, what are the factors that would make them difficult to introduce?

Draw up a list of these further topics. Then work with two or three other students and discuss the issue(s) in which you are most interested.

Optional follow-up: Writing

IELTS

TASK 6 Write a short essay (250–300 words) giving your views on one of the aspects of urbanisation that you have discussed during this unit. Limit yourself to 40 minutes' writing.

Share your writing with other students in the class.

UNIT 2 Differences between academic cultures

This unit aims to develop listening skills by:

1. introducing Macrostrategy 2, Monitoring
2. identifying markers of quotations (direct speech)
3. looking at the different meanings of 'or'
4. practising the use of markers of conclusion
5. encouraging critical thinking about academic culture.

MACROSTRATEGY 2 MONITORING

Monitoring – which means *checking* or *observing* – plays an important role in effective listening. When you are reading, you can always go back and read something again if you find it hard to understand. But listening is more difficult in this respect. In a conversation you may be able to ask the speaker to repeat or explain, but that is not so easy in a lecture.

On the other hand, you can expect the lecturer to keep more or less to the same subject. But there will also be points where the lecturer 'changes direction' – for example, presenting contrasting opinions on the subject, or giving examples that contradict each other.

Monitoring includes asking yourself the questions:

- Have I heard that correctly?
- Have I understood what the speaker meant?
- Have I understood why the speaker said it?
- Has the speaker changed topic?
- What is the speaker going to say next?

Monitoring

IELTS

TASK 1   Listen very carefully to the text that the teacher is going to read out. There may be one or two words you don't recognise, and points where you have to change your mind about the meaning. Concentrate on the monitoring questions shown as bullet points above.

Make notes on what you hear. When the teacher stops, say what you think will come next.

PRE-LISTENING

Introduction to the lecture topic: Academic cultures

Reading

Read the extract below and ask the teacher to explain any words that are unfamiliar or unclear.

> In one sense, culture is taken for granted. It involves assumptions, ideas and beliefs which are often not articulated, and members of a culture may not be explicitly aware of such assumptions. Culture is a pattern of normal ways of doing things, what people expect and how people interpret situations in which their expectations are not met. Academic culture, then, refers to this taken-for-granted system for carrying out academic matters.
>
> (Jin and Cortazzi 1996: 206)

Pre-listening discussion: Content

One example of the 'academic matters' that Jin and Cortazzi mention is the concept of an *essay*, and the essay is at the centre of the lecture to which we are going to listen in this unit. Here are some questions to talk over in preparation for listening.

1 What is an essay? What other kinds of writing do you expect to have to do at university?
2 How long do you expect an essay to be?
3 Does an essay have any of the following:
   a) a contents page
   b) a summary
   c) headings and sub-headings
   d) a list of references?

Pre-listening discussion: Language

Among the expressions you will hear in the lecture are:

on the face of it = at first sight, initially

a bit cross = rather annoyed

the proverb *Pride comes before a fall*.

What is the equivalent of that proverb in your language?

The lecturer

The speaker is Olwyn Alexander, who is originally from New Zealand and now works at Heriot-Watt University in Scotland. In her talk she discusses her experience of being a student in those two academic cultures, New Zealand and Britain, which you might expect to be very similar. Her talk centres on a conversation with one of her tutors on a postgraduate course in Britain, which showed her how different his expectations of an essay were from hers.

She mentions two authors, Alexander Pope and Charles Lamb, who were leading writers of literary essays in England in the eighteenth and nineteenth centuries, respectively.

Like Adrienne Hunter in Unit 1, Olwyn Alexander helps her listeners by:

1 outlining the structure of what she is going to say
2 listing the points in each section of her talk.

In addition, she:

3 dramatises her point by quoting the words she remembers using and hearing in the conversation with her British tutor
4 draws conclusions – the 'lesson' she has learnt from her experience.

Lecture language: Quotations

When she is recalling her conversation with her British tutor, Olwyn Alexander uses the informal expression 'says I' (instead of 'I said') to quote her own words.

Lecturers use various markers to make clear when they are quoting other people's words.

For example, in speech they use:

- *they said ..., she replied ..., he asked ..., (X) was his answer*

And in written texts they put:

- *Quote* or *Open quotes* at the start, and *Unquote* or *Close quotes* at the end
- reporting verbs like *write, claim* and *conclude*.

Lecture language: Drawing conclusions

Common expressions for the 'point' of an example or illustration include:

what this shows / reveals / illustrates is ...

the lesson we can learn from this is ...

the moral of the story is ...

the point of this is ...

FIRST LISTENING

As you listen, practise applying the Macrostrategies of Predicting and Monitoring by following the instructions below.

Predicting

You have discussed what an essay is and what makes it different from other sorts of writing. Think about that again before you listen.

Monitoring

As you listen, notice and use the ways in which Olwyn Alexander makes it easier for listeners to follow her talk by:

- outlining the structure of the talk
- signposting the separate sections and points within sections
- marking the direct speech in the conversation with the tutor
- listing her conclusions from the experience.

Listening and note-taking

TASK 2 You are going to hear the complete lecture, which lasts about 8 minutes. Don't worry if you don't have time to note down all the information you need to. There will be a second chance later.

Below is a note-frame to help you follow the talk. You can make notes on a blank sheet of paper, if you prefer.

Differences between academic cultures

Outline:

    1

    2

two cultures

OA's experience

diff's between Sciences and Arts

OA's story – 'essay'

The lesson

TASK 3

Oral summary

After the first listening, work with another student. Use your notes and take it in turns to summarise the talk under the six headings in the note-frame.

SECOND LISTENING
Detailed note-taking

The teacher will play the lecture again. Look and listen carefully for points where, during the first listening:
- you did not catch what Olwyn Alexander said
- you didn't have time to note all the details the first time
- you misunderstood what she said.

Comparing notes

With a partner, compare the *content* of your notes.
- Do you agree how many points Olwyn Alexander mentioned under 'the lesson' at the end of her talk?
- If you missed any other points, has your partner made notes on them?
- If there were points (or words) that neither of you could understand, see whether others in the class can help.

Then compare the *form* of your notes. For this you will need to put them side-by-side. Look for differences between the ways in which you have used:

- abbreviations
- symbols
- layout (such as linear notes or spider's web)
- emphasis (such as underlining or capital letters).

A sample set of native listener's notes is shown on page 138 in *Transcripts and sample notes.*

AFTER LISTENING
Post-listening: Focus on language
The meanings of 'or'

The word 'or' can be used in at least four different ways, shown by the examples below.

On the right are four uses (A–D) of 'or', in jumbled order. Match the use with the relevant example.

1 *Are you doing physics **or** chemistry?*	A an alternative word with the same meaning
2 *One of the problems is assimilation, **or** the merging together of words in speech*	B an alternative choice or possibility
3 *She's Malaysian – **or** at least so she says*	C self-correction
4 *He's doing a PhD, **or** rather an M.Phil*	D hedging/uncertainty

Fast speech

Lecturers vary their speed of speaking – on different occasions, in different parts of the same lecture, and even within the same sentence. But saying something quickly often shows the speaker thinks it is *less important* – like using brackets in writing.

When English words are spoken at natural speed in connected speech, their pronunciation tends to change. Many of these changes follow regular 'rules' of rapid speech. Since speed of speaking is one of the principal causes of listening difficulty for international students, it's important to practise understanding these patterns.

There are two main ways in which words change their pronunciation: *assimilation*, when neighbouring words merge together, and *reduction*, where a sound is omitted. Here are some examples, with their common approximate pronunciation on the right.

assimilation	*flat pack*	'fla(p)pack'	
	black bird	'bla(g)bird	
	London Bridge	'londo(m)bridge'	
	nice shot	'ni(sh)shot'	
reduction	*I would tell him*	'I'(d)telim'	
	she is going to see her doctor	'she'sgonnasee'adoctor'	
	he would never have lied	'he'dnevravlied'	

Transcript listening
Section 1: Fast speech and 'or' expressions

:IELTS

TASK 4 You will now hear the first part of Olwyn Alexander's talk again. The gaps in the text represent either expressions introduced by the word 'or', or examples of faster natural speech.
1 Try to fill in the gaps.
2 In which ways was Olwyn using the 'or' expressions?

    hello / my name's Olwyn Alexander / I teach at a university in the United Kingdom / and I help / overseas students to improve their academic writing skills / I often ask the students to reflect on the differences in education culture between the system in their countries

5 and the UK / I think this helps them to critically examine some of the assumptions they make about uni... about writing at university / today I'm going to share with you my own reflections about differences in education culture / and _____
which I hope will show you what I mean by education culture / and

10 how important it is to be aware that differences exist when you move from one education culture to another /

the two cultures I'm going to talk about will seem on the face of it to be very similar / they are New Zealand and the United Kingdom / New Zealand was a colony of the UK / so English is the main language in

15 both countries / and the New Zealand education system is based on the British one / it has primary secondary and tertiary level education / with the tertiary _____ level organised around departments / grouped into schools / _____ / actually I've got experience of studying in several faculties / science and arts in

20 my first degree / and social science much later on / in my postgraduate study / my first degree was in chemistry and physics / but was modular / and I was able to take up to five modules outside the School of Science / I chose to study English literature / in the School of Arts and Humanities / I don't suppose you could imagine / two more different

25 subjects / _____ between

science and arts and this was an opportunity to keep going with both of them / as you can imagine / there are a lot of differences in the way that science and arts students write / and what they have to write about / sciences focus on activity-based skills such as describing

30   procedures, defining and solving problems / the arts are more interested in seeing that students can analyse several sources / from different authors / and synthesise these into their writing / science undergraduates write reports / with well-defined sections and subsections / with headings / and arts undergraduates write essays /

35   my story concerns that little word *essay* / and my understanding / _____ / in the two education cultures I'm going to talk about / first I just need to tell you a little bit about these two cultures / they were both called social science / some years ago I studied for a Masters degree in Applied

40   Linguistics / here in the UK / in order to understand more about English and learn how to teach it more effectively / several years before I'd begun to study a postgraduate diploma in teaching English as a foreign language / in New Zealand / but as it happened I wasn't able to complete that diploma / now the content of these courses

45   was very similar / they had the same kinds of modules and the same _____ reading lists / however as I discovered / the writing tasks were quite a bit different / and the view of what constituted a successful outcome was also / quite different /

Section 2: Showing direct speech
In this section, some of the gaps represent expressions where Olwyn Alexander showed that she was quoting directly what she or the tutor had said. Others are examples either of rapid speech or 'or' expressions, as in Section 1. Again, try to fill in the missing words.

      to get back to that little word *essay* / you might like to think for a
50   moment what an essay is / how would you write if you were asked to write an essay? / for me an essay's a logically connected piece of prose / which sets out to make a number of points in order to answer a question / this question's usually posed in the introduction and answered in the conclusion, on the basis of evidence drawn from the

55   points made in between / _____ / I'd written a number of essays for my TEFL diploma course / and got rather good marks / but pride comes before a fall / on the Applied Linguistics course the first writing task was an essay / just to see if we knew how

to write one / 'no problem' I thought / 'I know what one of those is' /
60 I struggled a little with the writing, as I do with all writing tasks / even
though I think I am quite an experienced writer / but what I produced
I thought was a reasonable attempt at an essay / however I got quite
a low mark for it / and I went to my tutor to find out why /
_____ / 'what you wrote was quite different
65 from all the other students' / 'in what way?' – _____ /
'well it was like an undergraduate essay' / an undergraduate essay?
/ I was a bit cross / 'undergraduate? / Alexander Pope wrote essays /
Charles Ra… Lamb wrote essays / were these undergraduate too?' /
you can see I had quite a good opinion of my ability to write at this
70 time / 'what did the other students do?' _____ / 'well
theirs were postgraduate projects with sections and subsections /
with headings' / 'oh' says I / just a little ironically / 'you want me to
make it look like a scientific report?' / 'well yes' / _____ /
I discovered later in my course that social science in the UK / and
75 possibly also in New Zealand _____ /
was suffering from what was called *physics envy* / _____
_____ / researchers in the so-called soft sciences
envied the hard sciences for their ability to run experiments / control
variables / and produce reliable data / and they attempt to introduce
80 the scientific method into their research / and report it in scientific
ways / hence the style of the essay I had to write / which should really
have been called a *project* all along /

Section 3: Conclusion – 'My first lesson'
In this final section some of the gaps are points where Olwyn
Alexander explains her conclusions. Others are 'or' expressions.

of course the contrast is not nearly as simple as I'm making out /
but I don't really have time to go into that today / but this was my first
85 lesson that different education cultures had different ideas about ways
to communicate within their cultures / even though on the face of it
they seemed as if they should be very similar / I learned a number of
things from this, I think / _____ / _____
the dictionary definition of a word / _____
90 _____ / may not necessarily be
very useful when you move to a new education culture / _____
_____ the necessity of paying attention to your audience
/ and finding out about their assumptions / particularly if they're going

to grade your work / _____ that it's essential for me to
95 teach my writing class students / how to research the academic
cultures they'll be studying in / and pay attention to the way that
culture chooses to communicate its knowledge / and its research
results / there'll be differences related to the level of study /
undergraduate _____ / the particular discipline /
100 sciences _____ / and even the
particular subject and department that the course is taking place in /
_____ across the whole of academic
/ um / education and find _____

Troubleshooting

Some of my students in Edinburgh have had difficulty with the very
last words in the lecture. Were you able to write them in accurately?
What do they mean?

Were there other points in the talk that the class as a whole had
problems with? If so, your teacher will replay them and help you to
analyse what made them difficult.

Post-listening: Focus on content

Being an outsider

Olwyn Alexander's story reflects her experience of attending
university courses in two English-speaking cultures and noticing
differences in their local conventions. In the light of her experience,
think about the extract below.

When an individual moves from one academic system to another, this movement
may be vertical (that is, from school to university in the same society), horizontal
(from a university in one society to a university in another society), or diagonal
(from school in one society to university in a different society).

(Coleman 1991: 16)

1 Was Olwyn's move from New Zealand to Scotland vertical,
horizontal or diagonal?
2 Which of those three types of move do you think is likely to be
most problematic?
3 Have you noticed any differences in expectations between the
academic culture in your home country and that of another
country? (For example, international students are often unsure
what to call their lecturers – 'Tony', 'Dr Tony', 'Dr Lynch', 'Doctor',
'Professor', 'Teacher'.)
4 Are there academic habits or conventions in your home country
that you think should be adopted in other academic cultures?

Critical thinking
Objecting to a mark

Do you think it would have been possible for Olwyn Alexander to make a formal complaint about the low mark for her essay? Can students do that in the academic culture where you are now studying?

Academic writing

Below is a text comparing the way Western and Chinese academics write up their research.

In the science reports written by Westerners, they normally give an introduction which reviews the research done by others – very wordy. When they discuss the new techniques or methodology, they put in quite a lot of irrelevant quotations from others and from their own previous writing. At the end of the paper they again give reviews and prospects and implications of their research. So their papers are quite long, with a lot of references.

But our Chinese writing is different. We don't have the introduction part. We just introduce this new method or technique, our thinking on this research, how it is used or processed, how effective it is for the project and the wider technical world, and how it can solve the problem. This is because people who read these journals already know the previous research and where the problem is. What they need to know is how to solve the problem. They won't read those review parts. They will just jump to the new part to read about what they want to know.

Chinese postgraduate student quoted by Jin and Cortazzi (1996: 212–213).

1 Is that Chinese student being critical of:
   a) Western writing
   b) Chinese writing
   c) both?
2 Which words in his text support the answer you have just given?
3 Do you agree with what he wrote?
4 There is usually a word limit, such as 2000–2500 words for an essay and 5000–6000 words for a project. Why not allow students to write as much as they can or want to?

UNIT 3 Teleworking and distance learning

This unit aims to develop listening skills by:
1. introducing Macrostrategy 3, Predicting
2. showing how to exploit importance markers
3. highlighting how definitions and explanations appear in speech
4. providing practice in listening to fast speech.

MACROSTRATEGY 3 RESPONDING

Being an effective listener to lectures involves not simply *receiving* what the lecturer says but also *responding* to it. *Responding* here means relating the lecture content to your knowledge and personal experience, and forming your own opinions. It requires asking yourself questions such as:
- Do I accept that what the lecturer is saying is true and relevant?
- Can I think of other examples that support – or don't support – what is being said?
- Do I think the lecturer's opinions are reasonable?

The topic of this unit provides a good opportunity for this sort of responsive listening. The lecturer summarises the advantages and disadvantages of teleworking and distance learning, both for the people involved – workers and students, employers and course tutors – and also for the community as a whole.

PRE-LISTENING

Introduction to the lecture topic: Teleworking and distance learning

Communication technology, especially email and the Internet, now makes it possible for some employees to work from home using telephone and computer. But teleworking does not suit everyone, as is shown by recent research.

Reading
Read the five research findings that follow, then discuss with a partner what the missing words could be.

1 Teleworkers can feel .... and may have trouble feeling they are part of a ....

2 Teleworkers are more likely to be .... about how well they are doing their job.

3 .... are more frequent when people are communicating by email and telephone.

4 Some teleworkers find that because there is no division between work space and home space, they are more likely to work .... hours and to find it difficult to .... the computer.

5 Teleworking can also create problems for the employees 'left behind' at the main office, who may feel .... of their teleworking colleagues.

> (Source: D. Moody and I. Steinberg. Training for teleworkers: How to make the most of the 'privilege'. *Training Journal* March 2002.)

Pre-listening discussion: Content

1 Does anyone in the class have experience of teleworking? Or do they know a friend or relative who is a teleworker? Ask them to tell the class what they know about the *advantages* from the employee's point of view.

2 Working with a partner, make a list of the pros and cons of *distance learning*, from the student's point of view.

3 What do you expect the lecturer will say are the benefits and costs for *society as a whole* if more and more people telework or study on distance learning courses? Again, make a list of the points for and against.

Pre-listening discussion: Language

1 What other terms do you know for *teleworking* and *distance learning*?

2 We have just seen three pairs of words for the positive and negative sides of something.

advantages	disadvantages
pros	cons
benefits	costs

Can you add any others to the list?

The lecturer

The speaker is Dr Ron Howard, an Australian who recently retired from the Institute for Applied Language Studies at the University of Edinburgh, where one of his responsibilities was the running of distance learning courses for teachers and learners of English. In his talk on teleworking, Ron Howard uses two techniques that are useful tools in the lecturer's repertoire.

- He uses *importance markers* to highlight the key points in his argument.
- He defines and explains *technical terms.*

Lecture language: Importance markers

One vital listening skill is the ability to recognise and exploit the importance markers with which lecturers underline or emphasise points in their argument. They can do so in any of three ways.

1 By speaking about the subject matter itself

The	central	problem	is	that ...
A(n)	basic	point		
One	essential	fact		
Another	key	issue	is	the ...
(etc.)	crucial	difference		
		(etc.)	(etc.)	

2 By speaking to the audience

It's	important	to bear in mind that ...
	(etc.)	
It's	worth(while)	...ing that ...

Remember that ...

Don't forget that ...

You shouldn't lose sight of the fact that ...

3 By speaking about themselves

I want to stress/emphasise/underline ...

My point is ...

What I'm getting at is ...

Lecture language: Definitions and explanations

Lecturers often need to introduce specialist or technical terms, in a way that will make their meaning clear to the audience.

(X)	is also known as	(Y)
	is also called	
	is what we might call	
Another term for (X)	is	(Y)
(X)	is usually defined as ...	(Y)
	might/could be defined as ...	

By (X)	I mean	(Y)
What I mean by (X)	is	(Y)
(X)	in other words,	(Y)
	that is,	
	or to put it another way,	
	i.e.	

FIRST LISTENING

Listening and note-taking

TASK 1 Dr Howard's talk lasts about 11 minutes. As you will hear, he does not begin with the usual introduction; instead he opens his talk by explaining some of the main technical terms he wants to use in the lecture.

1 On this first hearing, try to note down the main points. You will get a second chance to pick up additional information later. Make a conscious effort to exploit the two aspects of lecture language we have just discussed:
   - Pay attention to importance markers.
   - Listen out for definitions and explanations of technical terms.

2 While you are listening, think about your personal response by asking yourself these questions:
   a) Do you think that what Ron Howard says is true of your country?
   b) Can you think of other examples that support – or don't support – what he says?

3 On the facing page is a note-frame that you may want to use to help you to follow the talk.

As usual, you can choose to make your notes on a blank sheet of paper, without using the note-frame.

Teleworking (TW) and Distance Learning (DL)

Terminology

Occupations using TW

TW	**Adv's**	**Disadv's**
Worker		
Employer		
Society		

DL		
Student		
Tutor/ course organiser		

Conclusion

Oral summary

TASK 2 Work with another student. Use your notes to summarise the main points.

SECOND LISTENING

Detailed note-taking

Did you notice that Ron Howard indicated that some of the advantages and disadvantages were *more important* than others? Monitor that aspect of his talk as you listen again. Add details to your notes where necessary, to show the relative importance of the points.

Comparing notes

1 After your second listening, compare the *content* of your notes.
  - Have you included the same information?
  - If you missed certain points, has your partner got notes on them?

If there were points (or words or sections) that neither of you could understand, see whether others on the class can help.
2 Then compare the *form* of your notes. Look for differences between the ways in which you have used:
  - abbreviations
  - symbols
  - layout
  - emphasis.

AFTER LISTENING

Troubleshooting

Ron Howard used fewer list markers than the speakers in Units 1 and 2. That may have made it harder for you to decide how many points he was listing in each section. If so, the teacher can stop at the end of each section, for you to discuss how many points there were.

You can then compare your answers with Ron Howard's own notes, which are shown in *Transcripts and sample notes*, page 142.

Post-listening: Focus on language

These two activities involve listening to the talk again in sections, and reading the transcript.
1 Listen and look for the technical terms Ron Howard mentioned in his opening section (underlined in the first paragraph of the transcript). Do they match your answers to the questions on page 38 about terminology?

2 Then listen to the rest of the talk. Circle the <u>marker phrases</u> he used to point up the advantages or disadvantages he thought were more important than others.

Transcript: Teleworking and distance learning

<u>teleworking</u> literally means working at a distance / that is, far from the office or normal place of work / usually though not always this means working at home / but that's not to say that everyone who works at home is a teleworker / teleworking / also called <u>e-working</u>

5 or <u>telecommuting</u> / has come to mean specifically working at home but communicating with the office by telephone or computer link / related to teleworking is <u>distance learning</u> or <u>telestudying</u> as it can also be called / and much of what I have to say about teleworking also applies to distance learning and teaching /

10 there's been a rapid increase in the number of teleworkers and telestudents over the past ten years or so / naturally this growth in the number of teleworkers affects only certain occupations / workers involved include those in the information sector especially / but also business professionals and scientists / and also teachers / in some

15 cases people are being persuaded or even forced to become telecommuters / but often they choose to do so themselves / why do people choose to work at home? / well there are a number of advantages for the worker / and also for the people who employ them / and for society in general / let's look at these /

*

20 first of all what are the advantages for the worker? / I would say the main advantage is that less time is spent commuting / that is travelling to and from work / someone working in a big city like London can easily spend an hour or more travelling to work / and the same amount of time returning home / two or three hours a day can therefore be

25 saved / and this is time that can be spent in more profitable ways than sitting in a train or car / commuting is quite stressful / and teleworking eliminates that stress / not having to travel saves not only time but also money / bus or train fares can amount to hundreds of pounds a year / motoring costs are also high / working at home

30 can be more convenient than working in an office / work time can be scheduled to suit the worker rather than the boss / breaks can be taken as and when needed rather than according to fixed schedules / and it's generally pleasanter working in the comfort of your own home

/ there's no need to dress up and so on / the choice of a place to live

35 no longer depends on nearness to the office / less expensive and more attractive areas far from the city now become a possibility / finally people who can't leave home for any reason can work as telecommuters / for example those with disabilities / or the need to look after small children or elderly parents /

40 recent surveys have shown that 68% of people who telecommute want to continue / but / 32% want to return to central office working / why? what are the disadvantages? for one thing the worker may have to equip his home at his own expense / this means buying a computer and peripherals such as a printer and perhaps also a fax machine /

45 heating and lighting bills are likely to be higher / and there's also the question of insurance / these costs have to be set off against the savings from not having to travel / even if the employer pays for the equipment / home working makes a demand on space / a spare bedroom may have to be converted into an office /

50 more importantly perhaps someone working at home will not have the backup that can be taken for granted in an office / technical staff to troubleshoot computer problems will not be on hand for example / there's also a loss of social support from co-workers / there may be many distractions in the home / from a partner or from young children

55 / there'll be many temptations to put off work in favour of more agreeable alternatives or even of domestic chores / the teleworker needs to be highly motivated / or at least extremely self-disciplined / many teleworkers are self-employed or part-time workers, and so they don't have the advantages of full-time employees / for example paid

60 leave, accident and sickness cover / they may also need / they may also be paid less / in other words they're in danger of being exploited by less scrupulous employers keen to take advantage of the situation /

*

so what are the advantages and disadvantages for the employer? / the major advantage for the employer is saving on costs / the employer

65 doesn't need to provide workspace and equipment / there are savings in running costs such as rates, electricity, catering / and telecommuters in some cases receive lower payment for their work /

surveys seem to show that teleworkers are more productive than their counterparts / one study suggests that they're 20–45% more efficient /

70 so for a smaller outlay of money an employer can obtain more product and therefore greater profits /

on the other hand, the employer can't easily supervise what the workers are doing / he or she may feel it necessary to visit the workers at home on a regular basis / this involves time and money / 75 an additional issue in these home visits is that workers may resent what they see as intrusion into their personal lives /

converting to teleworking obviously requires a great deal of reorganisation / lack of experience in the field means that the employer will either need to engage an expert to help in the reorganisation / or 80 risk making costly mistakes /

*

the move to teleworking has implications for society as a whole / if workers no longer need to commute there'll be less traffic on the roads, and therefore fewer accidents and less pollution / since the disabled and others can now work as telecommuters there may be a 85 reduction in unemployment / and if workers are more satisfied society as a whole will be happier / with the poss... with possible reductions in illness and crime /

again there are possible disadvantages / with many people working at home there may be greater consumption of electricity, gas / finally, 90 as I've already pointed out / teleworking is not possible in many occupations / building workers, street cleaners, shop assistants, and many others will have to continue to work outside the home / and this may lead to dissatisfaction and resentment /

*

let's now consider briefly distance learning / in many ways it's parallel 95 to teleworking with the same advantages and disadvantages / convenience is again the main advantage for the learner / especially for those who live in remote areas / for example in the outback of Australia or the Highlands and Islands of Scotland / it also benefits those who cannot easily attend a university or college for other 100 reasons / such as disability / telestudying also allows people to choose a course which isn't available locally / people with a full-time job can combine work with study by doing a distance learning course / this has obvious economic benefits / in addition a distance learning course may be cheaper than a conventional one / as with teleworkers, 105 distance students can please themselves when to do coursework and are not forced to study at fixed times /

one disadvantage is that a distance learning course usually takes longer to complete than a face-to-face course / this may lead to loss of motivation and 'drop-out' / or failure to finish the course / as with teleworking distractions in the home may be a problem / it can be

110 difficult to find the quietness needed for study away from children or flatmates / television, music, conversation are all too easily available / telestudents need to be at least as highly motivated as teleworkers /

perhaps even more so than work / learning is dependent on other people / both tutors and fellow students / feedback from tutors is

115 essential / and tends to work best if immediate rather than delayed / students learn from each other / not only from books and teachers / so the lack of support from tutors and students is important / so is the lack of library and other facilities /

finally some subjects are less suitable for home study / languages for

120 example / learning to communicate / which after all is the principal aim for most language students / demands the presence of others /

*

if tutors on distance courses work at home they benefit in the same ways as teleworkers in general / even if they work in an office they'll still enjoy some of the flexibility of home working / at the same time /

125 tutors have a managerial role / and just as managers in business / may find it difficult to supervise employees adequately / distance course organisers have to take particular care with accreditation / the absence of face-to-face contact interferes with the giving and receiving of feedback / which is so vital to teaching and learning / printed materials

130 need to be specially written to try to overcome this loss / although such technological aids as audio / and videoconferencing can help / it's arguable that nothing can replace a good teacher in a classroom /

*

so to sum up / many of the advantages have corresponding disadvantages and vice versa / but the drawbacks can often be

135 overcome by careful planning / the balance of advantages and disadvantages will obviously depend on the individuals and the situations concerned / teleworking and telestudying will never completely replace conventional work and study practices / both types of work and study have their place / perhaps the ideal is to

140 combine the two / working or studying at home / but with regular visits to the office or classroom /

Post-listening: Focus on content

Responding

1 Look back now to the notes you made for the Pre-listening questions 2 and 3 on page 38. Are there any other points that Ron Howard has not mentioned which you think are important?

2 Having heard the lecture, discuss the two points you considered on page 40:
   a) Do you think that what Ron Howard said is true of your country? If not, why not?
   b) Can you think of other examples that support – or don't support – the points he made?

Discussion

1 Ron Howard said some subjects are less suitable for distance learning courses. Do you think your own subject can be successfully studied at a distance?

2 He mentioned the positive environmental effects of teleworking, but did not go into detail. Discuss what benefits could result from more of us teleworking.

3 Of the three lectures you have heard so far – on urbanisation, academic cultures and teleworking – which do you think was the clearest? What made it so?

Role-play

Work with a partner. One of you takes the role of an employee who wants to telework from home; the other plays the employee's boss. The employee tries to persuade his/her boss that it would be a good idea, but the boss is reluctant. Both of you have to give clear reasons for your opinion.

Optional follow-up: Writing

As you heard, Ron Howard did not begin his talk with the usual introduction; instead, he moved straight to a definition of terminology. Write a short introduction (50–75 words) that he could have used to outline for the audience the areas he would be covering in his talk.

You can use the transcripts for Lectures 1 and 2 to guide you, as well as the signpost markers on pages 19–20.

UNIT 4 Language strategies for awkward situations

This unit aims to develop listening skills by:

1. introducing Macrostrategy 4, Clarifying
2. focusing on expressions of contrast
3. looking at how to exploit the information in a handout
4. providing practice in understanding rapid speech
5. developing an awareness of politeness strategies used by speakers.

MACROSTRATEGY 4 CLARIFYING

In a conversation, when someone says something we can't hear, we ask them to say it again. If we don't understand what someone says, we ask them to explain what they mean. This process is called clarification.

In a lecture, it's more difficult to get points clarified, because of the more public nature of the talk and because there may be dozens of listeners with potential questions. How lecturers and students deal with this problem varies from place to place. Let's start by comparing experiences.

1. In the country (countries) where you have studied, which of the following is expected?
   a) Students will not ask questions about the lecture.
   b) Students ask questions straight away, as soon as they need something clarified.
   c) Lecturers make 'pauses for questions' once or twice during the lecture.
   d) Students ask questions at the end of the lecture.
   e) Students go to the lecturer's room later to ask questions.
2. Which of those options, a)–e), do you think is the most effective, from the listeners' point of view?
3. Have you found that students are reluctant to ask questions? If so, why?

Whatever the local convention about asking questions is, it's important to think carefully about exactly what you need to get clarified. When you ask a question, you can help the lecturer to give the information you need by making clear whether the problem was due to:

- not hearing what the lecturer said
- not understanding what the lecturer meant
- not seeing the connection between different parts of what was said.

Clarifying expressions
Not hearing what was said
I didn't catch the word you used for …(X).
I didn't hear what you said about …(X).
I didn't catch what you said just after/before you talked about …(X).
What was the term you used for …(X)?

Not understanding what was said
I didn't get what you said about …(X).
I've not quite grasped what you said about …(X)
I'm not really clear about (X). Could you give us an example?

Not seeing the connection
I don't quite see how (X) relates to (Y).
I can't really see the link between (X) and (Y).
I don't see why (X) is relevant to (Y).

Even if you find it difficult to ask the lecturer, you can adapt those expressions to ask another student to clarify the point you are unsure about.

The way to make Clarifying most effective is to combine it with the macrostrategy of Monitoring. Monitor what you are confident you have understood as the lecturer is speaking, and listen out for points where you don't catch or can't understand what the lecturer says.

To help you to ask for clarification, make sure you show in your notes where you have missed or not fully grasped something – for example, by using a couple of question marks (??). Then ask for clarification when you have the opportunity. We will be practising that later in this unit.

PRE-LISTENING

Introduction to the lecture topic: Language strategies for awkward situations

We all encounter situations in our daily lives which are awkward [difficult or embarrassing]. The lecturer in this unit discusses how we can use language to maintain good relations with other people and to avoid offending or annoying them.

Notions such as 'politeness' vary from culture to culture. There are even differences in what is considered 'polite behaviour' between different parts of the same language culture. For example, in the English-speaking world, it is said that North American and British people differ in the degree of directness they use when asking people to do things for them.

Pre-listening discussion: Content

Imagine you are in a shop looking at clothes. One of the assistants approaches you and asks 'Can I help at all?' You don't think you need her help. Which of the following expressions do you think would be appropriate responses to the assistant's offer?
1 No.
2 No. Please leave me in peace.
3 Don't worry about me.
4 No, thanks.
5 No, not yet.

6 When I want your help, I'll ask for it.
7 I'm just looking.
8 Not for the moment, thanks.
9 I'd really appreciate it if you went away.
10 No, please find another customer to talk to.
11 No, not at all.
12 No, I'm fine.

Of course, all of those expressions are *possible*, in the sense that all of them are grammatically correct. But some are less acceptable than others. Number 6, for example, may appear extremely polite, but it's normally used in Britain to tell someone to stop interfering in your life.

Pre-listening discussion: Language

Metaphors
A *metaphor* is 'a way of describing something by comparing it with something else that has some of the same qualities. *She used a computer metaphor to explain how the human brain works*' (Cambridge Learner's Dictionary).

The lecturer refers to three military metaphors and explains them very briefly, so it would be a good idea now to check that you know their meanings before listening to the talk.

retreat

smoke screen

camouflage

Illustrations
He also mentions three species of animal showing different types of avoidance behaviour: pigeons, puppies and centipedes. If any of those words are new to you, check their meaning.

Expressions of contrast
A common technique used by public speakers is to say what something is not, before saying what it is, and you will hear several instances of this in the lecture.

this isn't really a case of (X)   *but of (Y)*

we are not trying to (X)   *but to (Y)*

that is not so much (X)   *as it is (Y)*

Alternatively, a lecturer may express the contrast the other way round.

this is really (Y),   *rather than (X)*

we choose (Y),   *as opposed to (X)*

we use (Y)   *in preference to (X)*

The lecturer

The speaker is Dr Hugh Trappes-Lomax, who teaches applied linguistics at the University of Edinburgh. His specialist field is discourse analysis, which deals among other things with the way that people communicate in conversation. Hugh grew up in the south of England, and then taught English and linguistics in Kenya and Tanzania for 15 years. As you will hear, he speaks a little faster in his lecture than the other lecturers we have heard so far. We will come back to this point in the Post-listening tasks.

Exploiting the information in a handout

Hugh Trappes-Lomax provides us with a handout to accompany his lecture. It contains three main elements:

- definitions of the key terms referring to language that avoids conflict
- examples of language used for that purpose
- quotations from authoritative sources.

Have a careful look through it now (pages 52–53) and discuss the following questions about the layout and presentation of the information.

1 Why are some words shown in _underlined italics_?
2 Why are some expressions shown in single quotation marks, and others in double quotation marks?
3 How is indentation used in the handout?

If you make effective use of the information in the handout, you should find it compensates for the fact that Hugh Trappes-Lomax speaks relatively quickly.

FIRST LISTENING

Listening and note-taking

TASK 1 The lecture will now play straight through, without stopping. Use the handout as you listen.

- Add your own notes and examples to complete the information there.
- Follow the text of the definitions and quotations.
- Make a note on the handout of points you would like to get clarified.

HANDOUT

Language strategies for awkward situations

"I'll think about it"

Why say "I'll think about it"?

tact   'a sense of what is fitting and considerate in dealing with others so as to avoid causing offence'   (Collins Concise Dictionary)

avoidance behaviour
e.g.

face   'a person's sense of self, of public self-image'

'simply by speaking we trespass on another's space' (Jenny Thomas)

avoidance strategies:

three military metaphors
1 retreat   silence

2 smoke screen   polite formulae

                ambiguity

                vague expressions

                avoid "no"

3 camouflage   nice words

euphemism 'a figure by which a less distasteful word or expression is substituted for one more exactly descriptive of what is intended'   (Shorter Oxford Dictionary)

'verbal hygiene' (Deborah Cameron)

products or services	second class on trains	=
	economy class on planes	=
	second-hand cars	=
	old house	=
	very small house	=
	price increase	=
work	boss	=
	employees	=
	to sack someone	=
body and its functions	toilet	=
	have sex with	=
	being old	=
	dying	=
political correctness	"chronologically challenged"	=
	"follically different"	=
	(AIM?)	
	children	
	with physical/mental problems	=
	with mental impairments	=
	generally, not "children", but	=

Conclusion: Does this matter?

'a language without euphemisms would be a defective instrument of communication'
(Burchfield)

Comparing notes

This time, focus on the points you have not fully understood.

- Can your partner clarify them for you?
- If there were points (or words or sections) that neither of you understood, compose a clarification question that will get the information you need.
- Ask those questions and see whether other students can answer them from their notes.

SECOND LISTENING
Points for clarification

Any points that still need clarification may become clear when you hear the lecture again. Listen a second time to the complete talk. Concentrate on the gaps, or areas of doubt, left in your notes.

Comparing notes

After listening again, compare your completed handout with the one on pages 146–147 in *Transcripts and sample notes*.

AFTER LISTENING
Post-listening: Focus on language
Clarifying

Now the lecture will be played again, stopping at the end of each section. If there is a point that you want to get clarified, ask your question and see whether another student can answer it.

IELTS   **TASK 2**   Follow the gapped transcript. The underlined spaces show where Hugh Trappes-Lomax draws attention to a point by using a contrast marker like those listed on page 50. Try to write in all the missing words.

Expressions of contrast

some time ago I was in a bicycle shop / looking for a new lock for my bicycle / the shopkeeper / showed me several / patiently explaining their advantages and disadvantages / none of them was quite what I wanted and eventually I said to the shopkeeper / 'I'll think about it /
5 thanks very much' / and left the shop / why did I say 'I'll think about it'? / not something more straightforward like / 'none of these is right' / 'they're too big' / 'they're too small' / 'they're too expensive' / 'I'll go elsewhere' / I think there are two reasons why I chose to say 'I'll think about it' / the first is I didn't want the shopkeeper to feel that his

10 products were not valued or that his time had been wasted / second /
    is that I didn't want to be the object of his possible annoyance or
    irritation / in other words / I didn't want him to feel bad / and I didn't
    want me to feel bad /

    *

    we have words for this general behaviour pattern of not wanting
15 ourselves or other people to feel bad as a result of / the interactions
    that we have have with other people / we talk about tact / which is
    defined in the Collins Concise Dictionary as 'the sense of what is fitting
    and considerate in dealing with others so as to avoid causing offence'
    / or we might equally call this / as many people do / *politeness*
20 *behaviour* / now notice that the definition of tact talks about avoiding
    giving offence / it is not talking about something positive that we do in
    order to make people feel better than they otherwise would / so here
    _____ the kind of behaviour we / get into
    when for example we console a friend whose cat has just been run
25 over / or compliment our partner on a very well-cooked meal /
    _____ positively make people feel better /
    but trying / to / avoid them feeling bad / so this is a negative kind of
    behaviour that I'm talking about / but the fact that it's negative
    _____ terribly important / it is / extremely
30 important / it is essential / to our self-preservation and to social
    cohesion / and for this reason avoidance behaviour is of great interest
    to / many different kinds of scholars / for example it's of interest to /
    biologists / uh who study avoidance behaviour as part of an animal's
    behaviour patterns / of aggression and defence / for example /
35 uh patterns of fleeing or freezing or producing various protective
    responses / we all know that when we walk through / uh Trafalgar
    Square the pigeons automatically fly away as our feet approach them /
    um we've all seen puppies who roll over on their backs and wave their
    tails between their legs / um when a larger dog comes along and takes
40 an interest in them / uh some of us may have seen what a centipede
    does when you touch it / it rolls up in a tight coil / thereby protecting
    itself from possible harm / now human beings do the same kind of
    thing but they do it in a more / sophisticated uh way probably / and
    for this reason sociologists, psychologists and social psychologists uh
45 take a great interest in avoidance behaviour / they see it as part of the
    means we use for maintaining good social relationships and our own
    and others' face / *face* has been defined as 'a person's sense of self,
    of public self-image' / linguists too take an interest in this kind of

behaviour / because they're interested in the communication tactics
50 and the language forms employed to avoid conflict / and maintain face
/ it has been said / by the linguist Jenny Thomas / that 'simply by
speaking we trespass on another's space' / so linguists are interested
in what language means we use to mitigate the effects of this
trespassing / the essence of linguistic tact is the choice of ways of
55 speaking which minimise unpleasantness, embarrassment or conflict /

*

the range of avoidance strategies can be summed up in three military
metaphors /

first metaphor / is *retreat* / under this strategy we avoid meeting the
person we keep away or we remain silent / or we avoid the subject
60 or change the subject / we talk about something else /

second metaphor is the *smoke-screen* metaphor / now under this
strategy what we do is use for example conventional politeness
formulae such as 'excuse me', 'would you mind?', 'sorry to bother you'
/ or we go in for a lot of vagueness and ambiguity / we try to be
65 imprecise / teenagers are very good at this when parents ask them
questions / 'who was that on the phone?' I ask and my teenage son
replies / 'a friend' / 'where are you going?' I ask / and he replies / 'out'
/ of course he could say a lot more but he chooses not to / he is
avoiding saying things which he thinks might cause trouble / and of
70 course we all make use of a variety of vague expressions which come
readily to hand as we speak / uh 'sort of' / 'like' / 'lots of' / 'kind of' /
and 'stuff' / words of that sort / I have just used one / and of course
one of the things we do try to avoid when we are speaking to people
is saying 'no' / uh 'no' is what sociologists call a *dispreferred response*
75 in most contexts / and so we try to avoid it / instead of saying no / we
say 'hmm yes and no' or 'that depends' or 'I suppose so' or 'up to a
point' /

third and last strategy is / the *camouflage* strategy / in this strategy we
choose nice words _____ ones / kind words
80 _____ honest ones / this is what we call
euphemism / defined in the Shorter Oxford English Dictionary as 'a
figure by which / a less distasteful word or expression is substituted
for one more exactly descriptive of what is intended' / the linguist
Deborah Cameron has a shorter and uh more / striking uh description
85 of euphemism / she simply calls it *verbal hygiene* / it's a way of
keeping ourselves linguistically clean /

*

there are various kinds of uh euphemism / um the example we started with is a euphemism / 'I'll think about it' / but it's a euphemistic utterance _____ _____ /

90 we all have a repertoire of such utterances to summon into use / when circumstances demand / 'you must come around one of these days' / we say or we hear / and this of course is not to be mistaken for a serious invitation / 'that'd be really nice' we reply or they reply / and this of course is not to be mistaken for an enthusiastic acceptance /

95 but most euphemisms are single words or short phrases which describe / people or things in a way which disguises / or camouflages things about them which make us feel uncomfortable or uneasy / here are a few quick examples / from a number of different domains /

one familiar category is expressions which make commercial products
100 or public services less bad than they really / seem less bad than they really are / for example examp… uh for example second class on British trains is called 'standard class' / sounds much better doesn't it? / economy class on planes is called 'tourist class' / second-hand cars have been described as 'pre-enjoyed' / an old house in an
105 advertisement may be called a 'period house' / a very small one may be called 'cosy' / a price increase is called a 'price adjustment' / all of these are clear examples of euphemistic language /

another area is the work area / in which the boss may be called the 'team leader' / or employees may be called 'human resources' / or to
110 sack somebody is described as 'letting them go' /

a third and very large category is to do with the body and its functions / the physical part of human nature / so / the toilet for example is referred to as the 'bathroom' or the 'powder room' / having sex is referred to as 'sleeping with' somebody or 'going to bed with' them /
115 being old is described as 'getting on a bit' or 'being a senior citizen' / dying / is called 'passing away' or humorously / 'pushing up the daisies' /

*

all these examples may seem amusing or even interesting / 'interesting' is itself a / uh a euphemism in some contexts by the way /
120 uh but hardly perhaps of great social significance / recently, however, euphemism has come out of the private domain of interpersonal communication / and moved into the public domain / it has become

political / so the last category that I want to mention I think is a very important category / it's one which is must... much discussed in the
125 media / and it is what is sometimes called politically correct language / the term political correctness is almost the opposite of a euphemism because it has become associated with absurdity and excess / so for example we have joke politically correct expressions such as 'chronologically challenged' which is supposed to mean old / or
130 'follically different' which is supposed to mean bald / these are absurd but the main idea behind this kind of linguistic behaviour is surely a good one / at least in intention / that groups of people should be made to feel socially included _____ and valued _____ / politically correct language / revolves
135 around issues of race, of sexual orientation and of disability particularly / uh let me take one particular example to do with children / children with physical or mental problems may be called 'exceptional children' / children with mental impairments are described as 'having learning difficulties' / children in general are often these days not called
140 'children' / which may seem to imply exclusion from the adult world of rights and independence / but they're called 'young people' or 'youngsters' or informally 'kids' /

does all this matter? / yes / we need euphemisms / the lexicographer Robert Burchfield says 'a language without euphemisms would be a
145 defective instrument of communication' / we need them but we also need to understand them and watch them carefully / we need to make sure / especially in the political domain / that we are the masters of them / not them of us

Troubleshooting
Speed of speaking
As we noted earlier, Hugh Trappes-Lomax spoke slightly faster than the other speakers so far. Did you find that was a problem? Or did the handout compensate for that?

Recognising stressed words
When listening to rapid speech, try to focus on the words that the speaker stresses. Listen again to the final 'paragraph' of the talk and mark in the stressed words.

Other problems?
Discuss now whether other aspects of the talk caused problems for people in the class. If so, the teacher will play that part again for you to follow the words in the transcript.

Post-listening: Focus on content
Discussion: Politeness and tact
1 The language we choose when speaking to someone reflects our respect for them or the closeness of our relationship. In this area, English probably allows you fewer choices than your first language does. The word 'you', for example, is used in English both when talking to a complete stranger and a close friend.
   a) In your language, how would you ask your course director or supervisor if you could speak to them for a few minutes about a problem?
   b) How would you ask a friend the same thing?
2 Have you been called 'sir' or 'madam' (or 'miss') in English? Where? In what situation would you use those words to other people?
3 Imagine a lecturer has been explaining a complex point to your class. You have not understood it. She then asks whether everyone has understood it. Would you admit that you had not grasped it? If not, why not?
4 Can you think of a recent situation in which you have not told the (whole) truth to avoid hurting someone's feelings?
5 How would you respond (in your language) to an invitation from someone that you don't wish to visit?

Critical thinking
Discuss the following questions in a small group and see what answers you come up with. Then ask the teacher to give an opinion.
1 Are there points that Hugh Trappes-Lomax made about English that would not apply to your own language and culture?
2 If you had the chance, are there any questions you would want to ask him?

Optional: Political correctness
Hugh Trappes-Lomax raised the issue of politically correct (PC) language towards the end of his talk.
1 How do you think people in your country would react to political correctness, as defined in the lecture?
2 Was he in favour of PC language, or against it, or somewhere in between? Read (or listen) again to the final section and find evidence to support your view.

UNIT 5 Targets for preventive medicine

This unit aims to develop listening skills by:

1. introducing Macrostrategy 5, Inferencing
2. showing how to exploit the speaker's stress on key words
3. providing practice in listening to fast speech
4. focusing on how speakers 'recycle' information.

MACROSTRATEGY 5 INFERENCING

Inferencing is really just a more academic word for *guessing*. For some reason, many people have a negative attitude to guessing. You hear them say '*Oh, I just guessed*', as if it were a less satisfactory way of dealing with a problem. In fact, guessing is an essential part of listening, even in our first language. It helps us to cope with situations such as when any of these happens:

- the information the speaker gives is incomplete
- we don't know the expressions the speaker is using
- we hear a familiar word, but used in an unfamiliar way
- we can't hear what the speaker is saying.

An efficient listener – especially when listening to a foreign language – regularly uses guessing as a main strategy. We are going to practise it in three short tasks.

Guessing from incomplete information

You will hear a mini-story read out (by the teacher). Listen carefully to the details. Where do you think the events took place?

Guessing at unfamiliar words

Sometimes we can infer the meaning of new words if they are made up of parts that we already know. For example, you can work out what a '*pencil box*' must be, even if you have never seen the expression before.

This time you will be given four words to work on. They are all in common use in a country where English is an official language. As you hear each one, write it down as it sounds and then try to guess what it means, from its parts.

Familiar words, unfamiliar meanings?

Now you are going to hear part of a real conversation between two people, Gus and Sue, who were talking about a single topic. The teacher will pause at five 'stopping points' in the conversation and ask you what you guess they are talking about. Most people find that they change their minds about the topic as they hear more of the conversation.

Listen to what Gus and Sue said. Each time the teacher stops, write down what you think the topic is, and the clue (word) that makes you think so.

stopping point	topic	clue
1		
2		
3		
4		
5		

PRE-LISTENING

Introduction to the lecture topic: Targets for preventive medicine

The proverb 'Prevention is better than cure' has its equivalent in many other languages. (Do you have one in yours?) The prevention of ill-health has gained greater importance as life expectancy, and therefore the number of older people, rises. According to World Health Organization figures, some 2 million deaths a year can be attributed to physical inactivity. In 2002, WHO issued a warning that a sedentary lifestyle – in other words, taking too little physical exercise – was among the 10 commonest causes of death and disability.

Reading

1 Read the text and underline any words you don't know.

'The habit of maintaining a healthy lifestyle, including regular exercise and a nutritious diet, ideally begins in childhood and we hope that parents and schools everywhere will use World Health Day to spread this message,' said Dr Gro Harlem Brundtland, WHO's Director-General. 'We should all be ready to move for health and to adopt healthy and active lifestyles. World Health Day is a call to action to individuals, families, communities, governments and policy-makers to move for health'.

Among the preventive measures recommended by WHO are moderate physical activity for up to 30 minutes every day, tobacco cessation, and healthy nutrition. In addition to individual lifestyle changes, governments and policy makers are also recommended to 'move for health' by creating a supportive environment for people. Among the community measures recommended are: implementing transportation policies that make it safer for people to walk and ride bicycles; legislating tobacco-free public buildings and spaces; building accessible parks, playgrounds and community centres; and promoting physical activity programmes in schools, communities and health services.

(adapted from WHO Press Release 23, April 2002)

2 Look again at the words you have underlined. Use the context (or the parts of the word) to guess their meaning. Check them with another student.

3 Choose one sentence that you think best summarises WHO's message.

Pre-listening discussion: Content

1 The text mentioned smoking, exercise and diet as targets for preventive medicine. Can you think of other issues of public health in your own country?

2 The lecturer we are about to listen to mentions the health hazards in developed and developing countries. Can you say which problems are common to both?

3 Which health problems are more typical of developing countries?

Pre-listening discussion: Language

Below is a list of words and expressions used in the lecture that may be unfamiliar to you. Look them up in a dictionary or discuss their meaning.

Words to do with **cause and effect**

(X) is a factor in (Y)   (Y) is due to (X)
(X) brings about (Y)   (X) is the chief offender in (Y)

Words related to **problems**

to tackle   prevalent
to suffer from   to deal with
to be faced with   one possible measure

Medical terms

nutritional deficiencies   *water-borne infections*
immunisation   *incidence (of a disease)*
birth control   *the median age of death*
addiction to   *medical practitioner*

Terms from **other technical fields**

flushing toilet   *pumping stations*

Background terms

Thames: the river that flows through London
Factory Acts: British laws controlling working conditions in factories

The lecturer

The speaker is Eric Glendinning, who comes from the south of Scotland. He has worked in a number of developing countries and is a specialist in teaching English for specific purposes, including medicine.

In addition to some of the lecturing techniques we have discussed in previous units (such as using importance markers and transition markers) Eric Glendinning uses three in particular that you should find helpful.

1 He makes effective use of his voice (for example by using emphasis, loudness and pauses) to highlight the key words and ideas in what he is saying.
2 He speeds up when he is giving less important information.
3 He uses two extended examples ('case histories') to illustrate a central point in his argument.

Lecture language: Stress on key words

When we write, we can show that part of a sentence is especially important by using underlining, capital letters, bold or italic print, or colour. When we speak English, we can achieve the same effect by stressing important words and ideas – speaking more slowly and loudly, and pronouncing them more carefully.

As we saw at the end of Unit 4, one common use of sentence stress in English is to contrast two or more words. Read the lecture examples below, and then say them aloud to another student. Underline the words you think a speaker would stress to make the contrast clear.

1 Governments may have to choose whether to use agricultural land to produce these crops for fuel or to produce them for food

2 We have to face the possibility that developing countries will continue to have greater infrastructural problems than developed countries

3 Local farmers are now getting two or even three crops of rice per year, where before they had difficulty getting even one

Lecture language: Fast speech

When a lecturer talks faster – and often quieter and less clearly – during parts of their talk, you can assume that the information is less important, or redundant. Here is an example from Eric Glendinning's lecture.

well having discussed the success of preventive measures in the past I would like to look now at the problems which remain for preventive medicine to tackle / and you'll note that these are no longer problems due to our external environment /althoughwecan'tdiscounttheproblemssuchas thechemicalpollutionofourfoodandtheair / but most of the problems which preventive medicine has to tackle today are the result of our own behaviour /

The words shown in smaller font were spoken more quietly, and I have run them together without the normal spaces between them, to show that they were enunciated less clearly.

When you are listening to a lecture, don't worry if some sentences are too fast, quiet or unclear for you to hear; they are probably ideas that the lecturer doesn't think are important. On the other hand, if you have problems with a lecturer who speaks faster than other lecturers *all the time*, then you could ask them to slow down a little.

Lecture language: Recycling – repetition, reformulation and exemplification

Lecturers can help to make information easier for listeners to understand and take in by **recycling** points and ideas. They do this in three main ways:

* *repetition* – saying something again, for clarity or emphasis

'it is wholly irresponsible / **wholly irresponsible** / to claim that human cloning is straightforward or even feasible'

* *reformulation* – saying something again in different words, especially when defining terminology (see pages 39–40)

'I think there are two reasons why I chose to say "I'll think about it" / the first is I didn't want the shopkeeper to feel that his products were not valued or that his time had been wasted / second / is that I didn't want to be the object of his possible annoyance or irritation / **in other words** / **I didn't want him to feel bad and I didn't want me to feel bad**'

- *exemplification* – illustrating an idea with concrete examples

'let's now consider briefly distance learning / in many ways it's parallel to teleworking with the same advantages and disadvantages / convenience is again the main advantage for the learner / especially for those who live in remote areas / **for example in the outback of Australia or the Highlands and Islands of Scotland** / it also benefits those who cannot easily attend a university or college for other reasons / **such as disability**'

If you recognise when a speaker is recycling information, you gain two advantages.
1 If you have already understood the point that is being made, you can listen less intensively when it is repeated or exemplified.
2 If you haven't fully grasped what the speaker meant the first time, you can use the recycling to try to get the point the second time.

Either way, recognizing recycling will help make you a more efficient listener.

FIRST LISTENING
Listening and note-taking

:IELTS   **TASK 1** As usual you are now going to hear the complete lecture. Note down as much information as you can, but there will be a second chance later to fill out your notes. As you listen, try to exploit the three aspects of lecture language we have discussed:
- listen for voice emphasis
- pay less attention to parts where the lecturer speaks fastest
- listen out for recycling of the main ideas.

At the start of his lecture, Eric Glendinning gives a very precise outline of the structure of the talk, and then clearly signals the transitions from section to section. There is a handout setting out his main points on pages 66–67.

Before you hear the lecture, take some time to think about Macrostrategy 5, Inferencing. There are bound to be some points in the lecture where you can't catch what is said or where you are unsure about the meaning.

In those cases, make a conscious effort to guess by using:
- the approximate sound of the words
- your knowledge of the subject
- the context in which the lecturer is speaking.

If you think they're important words, write them down as they sound, to check them later.

During the lecture, your teacher is going to **cover the sound** of some of the words, to help you to practise guessing!

HANDOUT

Targets for Preventive Medicine

Outline
1 Improvements in health in UK
2 Problems remaining
3 Targets for developing countries

1. Improvements in health in UK

Changes

Factors
- immunisation
- infant clinics
- screening measures
- the 'Sanitary Revolution'

2. Problems remaining

- Drug abuse

- Obesity

- Dental decay

- Old age

- Mental illness

3. Targets for developing countries

- Diet

- Tobacco & alcohol

- Population growth

- Disease

Choice of strategies — example: Malaria

Choice of strategies — example: Improved nutrition

Most effective strategy:

Inferencing

Were you able to guess any words you didn't know? Have you included them in your notes? If so, tell another student how you think they are spelt and what you guess they mean.

There will be another chance later in this unit to practise guessing at the spelling and meaning of new words.

Oral summary

⋮IELTS **TASK 2** Now take it in turns to summarise the points in the sections of the lecture, but don't show other students your notes yet.

SECOND LISTENING
Expanding your notes

Listen a second time. Keep an eye on your notes (and an ear on the lecture). Look and listen carefully for points where, during the first listening, you:
- did not catch what Eric Glendinning said
- didn't have time to make a note of all the information
- now realise you misunderstood what he said.

Comparing notes

After your second listening, compare your notes with those of another student.

Compare the *content* of your notes by doing and asking the following.

1 Look at the list of factors in the 'success story' of preventive medicine in Britain. Do you agree on which are the main factors and which are sub-factors?

2 Do you agree about the point of the two 'case histories' – malaria and nutrition?

3 If there were points (or words or sections) that neither of you could understand, see whether others in the class can help.

You can now compare your notes with the sample sets of notes on pages 151–152 in *Transcripts and sample notes*.

AFTER LISTENING

Troubleshooting

Chips, ships or sheeps?

Some students are puzzled by something Eric Glendinning said in the section on factors in the improvement of health status in Britain, when he was talking about the improvements in diet.

Perhaps you had the same problem? In your notes, have you included one of the expressions below, or something similar? These are all examples from students' notes in Edinburgh.

refrigerated chips

refrigerator chips

refuge-rated sheeps

refuge eighty ships

fridge or eighty chips

If you had difficulty with that expression, listen out for what Eric Glendinning actually said, when you hear and read Section 3 of the lecture.

Other problem points?

If there are parts of the talk that caused you particular difficulty during the first two hearings, discuss them now with your teacher. The class can then analyse the source of the problem when you reach that section of the talk.

Post-listening: Focus on language

This time we are going to work through the transcript in sections, using each one to focus on a different aspect of spoken language.

Section 1: Opening and outline of structure

Monitor the signpost markers that Eric Glendinning used to outline the structure of his lecture. Underline them in the following transcript.

>   well / good morning everybody / I'd like to talk to you today about the role of preventive medicine / first of all I'm going to discuss changes that have been brought about in our own society / and then / discuss some of the problems that remain for preventive medicine to
> 5 tackle / finally / if there's time / I'd like to contrast the the targets of preventive medicine in our own society / with the goals of preventive medicine in developing countries /

Section 2: Changes in health in Britain over the last century

This section contains examples of voice emphasis used to direct our attention to the lecturer's main points.

1 Eric Glendinning stressed certain words to contrast the two approaches to medicine. In the part of the section shown in bold print, underline the words you hear him stress more than others.
2 He used faster and quieter speech to show where information was less important – putting it 'in brackets', so to speak. That part has been shown in *smaller italic font*, with the words run together to represent faster speech, as on page 64.

>   if we look back a hundred years ago / in the United Kingdom / four out of ten children died in childhood / those who survived birth / uh
> 10 in the first few months of life were faced with diseases such as diphtheria, whooping cough, scarlet fever and tuberculosis / in the city slums the lower classes of society suffered from nutritional deficiencies / the deformities of rickets were quite prevalent / and all classes of society were vulnerable to water-borne infections / such as
> 15 enteric fever / that is, typhoid and paratyphoid / and cholera / from water supplies contaminated by sewage / today the population of the United Kingdom has doubled / and that's in spite of a fall of 50% in the birth rate / and only a very small minority of families suffer the loss of a child / now / **that we are healthier today and that we live longer**

20   **is not the result of curative medicine** / but of preventive medicine /
      I don't want to discount the important developments in curative
      medicine over the last sixty-odd years or so /
      forexamplethedevelopmentofuhsulphonamides / *andtheantibioticsespeciallypenicillin*
      / but the success / the success story / is really one which results from
25   preventive medicine /

Section 3: Factors in the success of preventive medicine in Britain

TASK 3   Before you hear this section, have another look at your notes. How
many factors do you have under 'the sanitary revolution'? As you
listen again, <u>underline</u> those factors in the transcript.

This section also contains the expression that students in
Edinburgh have found hard to understand (see page 68). It is shown
as a gap in the transcript. Try to complete it.

        let's look at some of the factors in this story / immunisation against
        diphtheria, tetanus, whooping cough and polio in the first year of life /
        protects the child from these diseases / the provision of infant clinics /
        health visitors / together with improved nursing standards and
30   midwifery standards / have helped reduce infant mortality / screening
        measures / *you'reprobablymostfamiliarwithmassradiography* / the screening
        for tuberculosis / screening measures help detect diseases in their
        early stages / before they've reached a dangerous stage / we can add
        to those preventive measures something which I will put under the
35   term '**the sanitary revolution**' / if you think of the industrial revolution
        as being what created the wealth of this country / the sanitary
        revolution created the healthy society that we have today / the
        sanitary revolution / I suppose really dates from the Public Health Act
        of 1875 / which resulted in piped water supplies / although ironically
40   one of the first attempts at improving the water supply in this country
        helped increase the incidence of cholera / the introduction of the
        flushing toilet in London increased the quantity of raw sewage
        entering the Thames / and the pumping stations for London's water
        supply were heavily contaminated as a result / not only piped water
45   supplies were important / but provision of cheap ⌈soap⌉ / people began
        to wash more frequently / public bath-houses were built and wash-
        houses / people started to wear cotton underclothes instead of wool
        / and cotton is more easily washed / more likely to be washed more
        more frequently / people enjoyed a better diet / due to such diverse
50   factors as _____

South American beef / New Zealand lamb / and so on / making available to all classes of society fresh fruit and cheap and fresh meat all the year round / birth control / the fact that children are now spaced out so that homes are no longer so crowded / uh as they were
55   / no longer so overcrowded / so that the factors which lead / which allow tuberculosis to flourish have been controlled / in the workplace Factory Acts have made working conditions much better / so that we're no longer subjected to the same industrial diseases which were prevalent in Victorian times /

Section 4: Problems – targets remaining for preventive medicine to tackle

:IELTS   **TASK 4**   Eric Glendinning closes this section on targets with a summary (review) of the five main targets, which should help you to check that you have noted the main points.

Concentrate on the gaps in the following transcript. Write in the missing words and, if necessary, guess what they mean.

60   well having discussed the success of preventive measures in the past I'd like to look now at the problems which remain for preventive medicine to tackle / and you'll note that these are no longer problems due to our external environment / *althoughwecan'tdiscounttheproblemssuch asthechemicalpollutionofourfoodandtheair* / but most of the problems which
65   preventive medicine has to tackle today are the result of our own behaviour / now let me list some of these problems for you they're on your handout / the first one is drug abuse / and I'm interested here / I'm concerned with the two main drugs / alcohol and tobacco / alcohol is a contributing factor in many road accidents
70   *somethinglikeathirdofallfatalroadaccidents* / in a third of these cases the driver / or one of the drivers involved / has alcohol in his bloodstream above the legal limit / think of the ravages of lung cancer / nine-tenths of lung cancer victims are smokers / and smoking of course brings
75   about not only lung cancer / but heart disease and bronchitis too / first problem drug abuse / our second problem is obesity / obesity brought about by _____ / and a lack of exercise / our Victorian ancestors had few of the labour / saving devices that we enjoy today *thatwethatweprofitfromtoday* / of which
80   the motor car is the perhaps the chief offender / lack of exercise / overindulgence in saturated fats / bring about obesity / and obesity leads to heart disease / back problems and so on / dental decay / dental decay is the most prevalent disease in the United Kingdom today / 36 million fillings are made every year by British dentists /

partially due to bad eating habits / but also due to poor dental hygiene
85 / all of these problems raise the question of how far should individuals
be free to harm themselves / when society has to deal with and pay
for the consequences / another major target for preventive medicine
today is the problems of old age / ironically the problems of old age in
our society are due in part to the very success of curative and
90 preventive medicine / if we think _____ / the
median age of death in the early Victorian period was 48 / and today
it's around 75 for men / so one of the main targets for preventive
medicine today must be to keep old people mobile / keep them out
of hospital / finally I've put down / as targets for preventive medicine /
95 mental illness / 5 million visits are made to doctors' surgeries each
year in this country by patients complaining of mental illness / these
then are the targets for preventive medicine today in the United
Kingdom / drug abuse / obesity / dental decay / the problems of old
age / and mental health /

Section 5: Targets for developing countries

Listen carefully to the part that has been shown in bold in the
transcript. What is the *contrast* that Eric Glendinning wanted us to
recognise?

Can you guess the spelling and the meaning of the words in the
gap? (Don't use a dictionary!)

100   now let's consider the problems of the developing countries / and
we'll start with some of the problems that we share with the
developing nations / **both the developing and the developed
nations suffer from bad diet / I've already talked about
overindulgence in saturated fats and carbohydrates in the West /**
105 **a problem of too much / in the developing countries the problem
is one of too little / problems which lead to undernutrition or
malnutrition / often / like ourselves / the problem is due not to
a lack of food / but due to an unbalanced diet / the lack of
certain components in the diet /**

110 other problems that are shared between the developing and developed
nations are the problems of tobacco addiction and alcoholism / I
suppose the third most obvious problem for preventive medicine
to tackle in the developing world / is the problem of uncontrolled
population growth / there's the danger that food supplies
115 _____ population increases /

and fourthly / there are problems of disease / malaria, leprosy, tuberculosis and of course HIV / where can we begin to tackle this problem / in the developing countries? / resources are limited / it is important that the most efficient strategy for success be employed as

120 early as possible /

let's consider / let's take as a case history / the problem of malaria / how do we eliminate malaria? / now there are three possible preventive measures / the first one would be to drain the marshes / *getridofthewetplaces wherethemosquitobreedsandthrives* / the second strategy

125 would be to kill the mosquitoes themselves / *spraythemwithinsecticide* / and the third strategy would be to give all the people living in the affected areas anti-malarial drugs to take / and notice / that we've / three possible strategies / and not one of them involves the medical practitioner directly / it's the task of the civil engineer to drain the

130 marshes / the important role in killing mosquitoes is played by

_____ / who goes round the houses spraying the walls and the ceilings / and the key figure in distributing anti-malarial drugs is _____ / finally there's the problem of the individual himself / who must / who

135 must take the drugs / *willheinfacttakethedrugs?* especially if these are anti-malarial drugs / especially if these are pressed on him by _____ foreign personnel / we can see the same / problem of choice of strategies / in the problem of _____ /

140 how do you get a better diet for people? / one strategy would be to introduce new crops / the task of _____ / another might be to irrigate / um and that's the task of the engineer / in some countries the major problem is that uncontrolled rain brings flooding / and that _____ and so on / the

145 answer there might be _____ or contour-terracing / and again / that's not the _____ of the medical practitioner / and **at the end of the day** again we have the problem of the individual / you can persuade the farmer to grow new crops / you can irrigate the fields to help farmers to do so /

150 but **at the end of the day** you must persuade the farmer and his family to eat them / and one of the major problems is persuading people to change their food habits / people are at their most _____ when they're concerned with filling their stomachs /

'At the end of the day' (shown in bold) is a common expression in spoken English. What do you guess it means, from the context you have here?

Section 6: Conclusion

In his final section, Eric Glendinning uses the expression 'for my money'. What does he mean?

155   we can see then / some of the similarities and some of the differences between preventive medicine in the developing countries and in the developed countries / now **for my money** the most effective strategy in both the developed and the developing countries is health education / health education must come first / you must

160 educate people to smoke less / to drink in moderation / you must educate people to change their food habits / to take a different diet / you must educate people to take prophylactic drugs / such as anti-malarial tablets / so / in conclusion we can see that / there are differences between the developing and the developed worlds in the

165 task of preventive medicine / but for both / the solution seems to be health education / thank you very much /

Post-listening: Focus on content

Responding to the lecture

Consider and answer the following questions.

1 What did Eric Glendinning have in mind when he talked about 'health education'? What forms does health education take in your country?
2 Do you agree with his list of priorities for preventive medicine in the developing world? Are there other problems that you think he should have addressed?
3 What measures has your government taken to reduce drug abuse and obesity? What alternative or additional policies would you suggest, to reduce them further?

Clarifying questions

Are there any points in the lecture that you are still unclear about? If so, compose a question that you would like to ask Eric Glendinning, for him to clarify what he meant. Then see whether other students or the teacher can give you the answer.

Critical thinking

Some people object to the common use of the expressions *developing countries* and *developed countries*. Why?

Would you prefer to use different expressions? Why are they better than the adjectives *developing* and *developed*?

IELTS

Optional follow-up: Reading/oral summary

TASK 5 Choose one of the ideas that you have found particularly interesting or important (or dubious) in the lecture. Search for a text on that topic on the Internet. One possible site is http://www.who.int

Then read and summarise the text in brief notes. Prepare a two-minute summary to give to the class at your next lesson.

UNIT 6

Cloning: The significance of Dolly

This unit aims to develop listening skills by:

1. introducing Macrostrategy 6, Evaluating
2. showing how reading input can help listening
3. providing practice at guessing the meaning of unfamiliar words
4. showing strategies for identifying negative and positive arguments
5. indicating how to recognise the stress on key words.

Dolly 1996–2003

©Najlah Feanny/CORBIS SABA

MACROSTRATEGY 6 EVALUATING

Students sometimes come out of a lecture saying things like '*I didn't understand any of that*' or '*What was that all about*?' They probably don't mean that they understood nothing at all, or that they have no idea what the lecturer was about. What they mean is that there were some sections of the lecture that they didn't grasp.

Evaluating your listening – that is, thinking about how well you have understood what someone has said – is an important strategy. Evaluating your success in listening can help you to:

- identify on which areas of knowledge you need to work
- identify which listening skills to practise more
- compare your listening skills in different subject areas of your course
- assess your progress in listening over time.

Evaluating involves deciding *what* was unclear and also *why* it was unclear. At the start of this course (page 11) we discussed four general factors that can make lecture listening difficult:

- the physical setting
- speaker
- subject
- language.

There is also a fifth factor – the listener. For example, you might be unable to take notes in a particular lecture because you are worried about something and can't concentrate.
What other 'internal' listener factors do you think influence your success in listening?

Evaluating your listening

Discuss your answers to these evaluation questions in small groups.

1 How good is your listening, compared to that of other people in the class?
   a) weaker than most
   b) about average
   c) better than most
   d) better than anybody else
   e) it depends

2 How about your note-taking? Which do you think it is?
   a) not as good as most people's
   b) about average for the class
   c) better than most
   d) best in the class

3 How much do you think you need to understand, in order to be able to take effective notes?
   a) less than 25%
   b) 25–50%
   c) 50–75%
   d) more than 75%

4 How much do you think you know about cloning?
   a) less than other people in the class
   b) as much as others in the class
   c) more than most in the class
   d) more than anybody else in the class

5 How much do you expect to understand of a lecture on cloning?
   a) less than 25%
   b) 25–50%
   c) 50–75%
   d) more than 75%

PRE-LISTENING

Introduction to the lecture topic: Genetic research and cloning

Reading

Read the text on the next page. When you find words that are unfamiliar or unclear, discuss them with another student or check them in a dictionary.

The term **genetic engineering** covers a wide variety of techniques that allow scientists to take a gene from one cell and insert it into another. When the gene enters the new cell, it can change the way the cell works or the chemicals that it produces. Genetic engineering can be used to improve crops by increasing the food value of a plant or its resistance to disease.

In a sense, this is not new. For thousands of years farmers have used planned breeding to manipulate the DNA of plants and animals, but this method is relatively slow and takes many generations to be effective. The advantage of genetic engineering is that it allows scientists to choose a specific gene and insert it into an organism, greatly increasing the rate at which the desired changes can be achieved. It also allows genes from one species to be introduced into a distantly related species – a process called **transgenics**. The use of transgenic animals could be the most significant development in the agriculture of the future. Transgenic animals are produced by inserting a gene into a fertilised egg when the embryo is still only a single cell. As the animal develops, the gene is reproduced in every cell of its body.

In time, genetic manipulation could lead to a completely new style of farming, as animals are engineered to carry genes and proteins with the potential to bring new treatments and cures for human diseases.

One potentially important development of genetic engineering is **cloning**, which involves a different form of genetic manipulation, **nuclear transfer**. For many people, the idea of cloning will always be associated with a sheep called Dolly – the world's first cloned mammal. Dolly was born at the Roslin Institute in Scotland in 1996 and was the subject of worldwide media attention throughout her life, particularly when people began to speculate about the possibility of cloning human beings. Many people believe that, even if human cloning is scientifically possible, it is unacceptable on religious and ethical grounds – and that cloning amounts to 'the scientist playing God'.

Dolly died in 2003, but the public debate about human cloning continues. In this Unit's lecture we hear a genetic researcher talking about the technique of nuclear transfer, the problems currently associated with cloning, and the importance of Dolly from the point of view of basic science.

Pre-listening discussion: Content

1 How would you define a *clone*?
2 The title of the lecture mentions 'the significance of Dolly'. Why do you think she was important?
3 What problems associated with cloning do you expect the lecturer to mention?

Pre-listening discussion: Language

The lecture includes a number of specialist terms which the speaker defines and explains. Here are some others, which are *not* explained in the talk.

mammary gland part of the organ that produces milk

surrogate mother /'sʌrəgət/ usually, a woman who agrees to have a baby for a woman who is unable to have children; here, it refers to a female animal carrying a foetus produced by genetic manipulation

gestation period of pregnancy

offspring child or children, usually of animals

placenta /plə'sentə / the body tissue that joins the foetus to the inside of the womb

oocyte /'uəsait/ egg before fertilisation

compromised used here to mean 'put at risk' or 'endangered'

xenotransplantation [the 'x' is pronounced like a 'z'] the transplanting of animal organs into human patients

The lecturer also uses two colloquial expressions:

fake   false or untrue

vibes   (short for 'vibrations'): emotional atmosphere or mood; feelings

The lecturer

The lecturer is Dr Harry Griffin, who works at the Roslin Institute near Edinburgh, where scientists cloned Dolly the sheep in 1996. Dr Griffin was born and brought up in the north of England, and has worked in England, the United States and Scotland. He is particularly interested in ensuring that the general public should gain a clear understanding of what genetic research can – and cannot – achieve.

Dr Griffin's lecture contains several features of lecture language that you have worked on in earlier units. Take advantage of them as you are making your notes, by focusing on:

1 the introductory outline of what he is going to cover
2 the way he marks new topics or sections by longer pauses
3 the strong stressing of key ideas
4 the definitions and explanations that follow many technical terms.

FIRST LISTENING

Listening and note-taking

You are going to hear the complete lecture, which lasts about 15 minutes. This time try to get as much information as you can on first hearing.

If you want to take notes unaided, you can simply use a blank sheet of paper. If you would like to use a note-frame, you have a choice of two formats. Have a look at the two note-frames below, then decide whether you want to use one of them, or to make your notes from scratch.

TASK 1 *Note-frame 1: Content-based*
Below is a list of the headings based on the content of the talk, of the sort Dr Griffin might have used in his own notes.

Note-frame 2: Language-based
On page 81 are the opening words of each section.

Note-frame 1: Content headings

Intro

Nuclear transfer

Speculation: Dolly

Other clones

Problems with cloning

Sources of problems

Human cloning?

Motivation for cloning

Importance of Dolly

Conclusion: balancing the picture

Note-frame 2: Section openings

Dolly the sheep was...

Dolly was created by a technique...

at first Dolly was a clone alone...

there are a number of well-characterised problems...

the reasons for the problems...

most of the public fascination...

our own motivation at the Roslin Institute...

given that the practical benefits... seem limited...

so in thirty years' time...

Evaluating your listening

1 How much of the whole lecture did you understand?
   a) less than 25%
   b) 25–50%
   c) 50–75%
   d) more than 75%

2 Which factors caused you most difficulty?
   a) the subject matter
   b) the technical vocabulary
   c) the speed of speaking
   d) the length of the spoken sentences
   e) the lecturer's accent
   f) lack of concentration

3 Were there other factors?

Evaluating your notes

1 How many of the main points do you think you have included in your notes?
   a) all
   b) most
   c) some
   d) none

2 Which do your notes show?
   a) less than you actually understood
   b) as much as you understood
   c) more than you understood

Compare your notes with your neighbour's. Whose notes are better? In what ways are they better?
   Remember the three rules from the Introduction to the course – *Be selective*, *Be brief* and *Be clear*.

SECOND LISTENING

Most students find that they need to listen to the lecture again, to check the number and exact details of the points made in each section, such as the number of stages in nuclear transfer, and the physiological problems associated with cloning.

Clarifying

Compose some clarification questions that you would like to ask Harry Griffin. If your class includes any students who are specialists in genetics, they may be able to clarify these points from their notes before you listen again.

Monitoring

Use your second listening to check your notes against what you hear, and focus on the points you would like to get clarified.

Compare notes with your neighbour again after the second listening. Sample notes are shown on pages 156–157 in *Transcripts and sample notes.*

AFTER LISTENING

Troubleshooting

Are there any parts of the lecture that people in your class found especially problematic? If so, the teacher can include further practice on them.

Post-listening: Focus on language

Harry Griffin's lecture provides a great deal of useful material for language study. We will be working through the talk transcript in sections (Sections 1–8), using each one to analyse a different aspect of spoken language.

....
:IELTS

Section 1: Outline of the lecture

TASK 2 Fill in the missing expression in the gap below.

> Dolly the sheep was the first mammal cloned from an adult cell /
> she was born on the fifth of July 1996 / and the announcement of her
> birth / uh about seven months later / started uh what has been an
> enduring fascination by the media and the public at large with all
> 5 things cloned / uh in this talk / I want to describe the technique by
> which Dolly was created and reflect uh on how the technology has
> developed / _____ / uh over the intervening five
> or six years / uh and then review very briefly the practical applications
> / uh of cloning / and try and separate / uh those that are likely / from
> 10 those that have uh / attracted a lot of speculation uh and media
> interest /

Why did Harry Griffin add that comment? (The answer relates to an area of lecture language that we covered in Unit 2.)

Section 2: Nuclear transfer

According to your notes, how many steps are there in the process of nuclear transfer? Harry Griffin used list markers for the first two. As you listen to this section again, fill in the markers in the gaps on the following page.

Dolly was created by a technique called *nuclear transfer* / and most of the manipulations involved are done by looking down a microscope and using micro-manipulators / _____ take an
15 unfertilised egg / and using pipettes to suck out / uh the maternal nucleus / _____ / the DNA is replaced / by inserting a cell / in Dolly's case uh from the mammary gland / back in place of the maternal nucleus that's been removed / the end-product of this sequence is in essence / uh a cell a body cell a mammary gland
20 cell uh within an egg / and this reconstructed embryo is activated and the two cells fused together / by a small electric pulse / and in a small proportion of cases / this reconstructed embryo begins to divide and multiply / just as a normal embryo would do / in the experiment uh in which Dolly was created / over 400 eggs were used / 277
25 reconstructed embryos were created and of these only about 10 per cent developed into blastocysts / that is the stage of embryonic development where there may be 100 to 120 cells / of the 29 uh cloned embryos that developed into blastocysts / they were implanted into 13 surrogate mothers / only one of which became pregnant /

Where could he have added other list markers, and what words could he have used?

Listen again to the final sentence in that section. Which word did Harry Griffin stress, and why?

.... *Section 3: Speculation about Dolly*
∷IELTS   **TASK 3** This section picks up an issue that Harry Griffin highlighted in his introduction – the contrast between media speculation about cloning and the concrete results of scientific research. He was keen to emphasise that cloning was a complex process, with uncertain outcomes.

As you listen to the section:
1 underline the negative words and expressions he uses to make clear that cloning is problematic
2 fill in the gap.

30   at first Dolly was a clone alone and there was a tremendous amount of speculation about whether or not the experiment could ever be repeated / or indeed whether we'd made a mistake / uh in creating Dolly not from an adult cell but from a foetal cell / and there were one or two suggestions that Dolly was simply a fake / all this
35 speculation came to the uh an end in the summer of 1998 when a

group in Hawaii reported uh the cloning of over 50 mice / and since
then uh research groups around the world have cloned cattle, sheep,
goats, more mice, rabbits / and pigs / and there's one example of a
cloned kitten / equally competent groups have tried to clone other
40 species and been unsuc… unsuccessful so far / as far as cloning rats,
dogs or monkeys / and overall the success rate of cloning is very low /
less than one per cent on average of cloned embryos
_____ / many cloned embryos uh fail to develop
at all / when they do develop to blastocysts some cloned embryos fail
45 to implant / and even when the surrogate mother becomes pregnant
carrying a cloned embryo / failures can occur throughout gestation /
up to and including birth /

Can you guess the meaning of the words you have written in the
gap?

Section 4: Problems with cloning
In this section Harry Griffin listed a number of problems, which
scientists have reported finding in cloned animals, but did not use
list markers. As you listen again, underline each problem.

there are a number of well uh / characterised problems with
cloning / in cattle and sheep / there's a tendency for the offspring
50 to be oversized / perhaps **up** to twice or more the size of normal
embryos uh when they are born / in mice / uh the cloned mice seem
to be a normal size / but the placenta can be twice or three times uh
normal size / problems persist uh **after** birth / cloned mice for example
tend to obesity / and there is one reported study uh of cloned mice
55 dying about two-thirds of the way through a normal lifespan / other
problems reported in clones uh include failure of the **lungs** to develop
/ or failure of the immune system uh a few weeks **after** birth / and
there has been uh questions raised about whether any clone is entirely
normal / and it's clearly going to be uh a long time before we can be
60 sure that cloned animals can be normal / studies need to be carried /
through uh a complete life**span** / which is clearly much easier than /
in mice than in a long-lived species like uh cattle /

Listen carefully again to the Northern English vowels in the words
shown in **bold**. How are words 'up' and 'lungs' pronounced? What
about 'after' and 'span'?

What do you notice about the expression 'there has been
questions raised about…' in line 58?

TASK 4 This next section provides good material for practising **guessing** how to spell words and what they mean. Some of the missing expressions are ones that you probably know. But what do they mean in this context?

the reasons for the problems associated with cloning
_____ whether or not the adult cell introduced

65 _____ is appropriately reprogrammed / normally uh embryos are produced by fusion of eggs and sperm / uh the DNA of which has been matured uh over years and months uh before the fertilisation occurs / the situation is very different with cloning / / because the DNA introduced into the oocyte uh is from a specialised

70 cell / a mammary gland cell for example may have thirty or forty thousand genes / but _____ / uh because they are / not used uh in the functioning of the mammary gland / what's being expected of that cell of that DNA / is that once it's transferred to / an enucleated oocyte those silent genes are reawakened / and

75 within a very short time / a matter of hours / they're expected to behave as they would do normally / uh in a / embryo created by fertilisation / it's not therefore surprising that if some genes are inappropriately regulated / uh come on during development uh too late or too strong / then uh normal development _____

80 _____ / most research groups working in this area now are concerned with trying to understand the basic mechanisms uh behind the reprogramming process / on the basis that if we can understand that / we can improve the success rates of cloning from the current one / perhaps one to two per cent in some

85 species / uh to make it a more viable uh more reliable process /

Section 6: Human cloning

We have seen that the way lecturers choose to stress certain key words is a powerful tool for making their meaning clear. In this section, (circle) the words that you hear Harry Griffin stress most.

most of the public fascination most of the media fascination / uh with cloning has been / along the lines 'is it possible to clone a human being?' / and certainly uh experience with a range of species suggests that in theory at least it should be possible to clone a child / whether

90 or not this is a sensible thing to do in the long term / uh is uh a matter of considerable ethical debate / certainly at the moment all the evidence / from experiments with animals suggests that this would be

a risky procedure / not just for the prospective child but also for uh the
mother carrying that child / and it would be wholly irresponsible using
95 the technology uh at its present state of development / for anybody to
attempt to uh clone a child /

Two of the stressed words in the last sentence would make a very
concise summary of Harry Griffin's attitude to human cloning.
Which are they?

Section 7: The motivation for cloning

Here Harry Griffin gave his views on the possible applications that
have been suggested for cloning. Listen for the way he used longer
pauses to mark the new topics in this section.

Show the breaks between topics by writing in a double slash //
where you hear a longer pause.

our own motivation at the Roslin Institute uh for cloning / or
developing the technology at least / was to produce / uh uh develop a
better way of genetically modifying farm animal species / cloning in
essence converts cells / cells that can be cultured / but cells into live
100 animals / and if those cells are first genetically modified / then the
clones produced from those cells will be genetically modified too / and
this approach has already been used to insert genes at a specific point
in the genome / uh milk protein genes / uh in order to produce human
proteins in the milk of transgenic sheep and cattle / and it's also been
105 used to delete genes / so in the case of pigs / for example / uh /
cloning has been used to delete a gene which is responsible for the uh
rejection of a pig organ by uh a human patient / the context here is
xenotransplantation / the possibility of using genetically modified pigs
uh to address the shortfall of / organs for transplant to human patients
110 / and it's very clear that if xenotransplantation is going to be successful
then it is the precision uh that uh the genetic modifications using
cloning uh can provide / that will make uh the technology ultimately
successful / cloning is normally / uh associated with the idea of
replicating or copying animals / and indeed there are research groups
115 and companies in Australia and New Zealand Japan / and the United
States uh trying to develop the technology to clone cattle and to
specifically uh copy the very best-performing animals / at the moment
the cost of producing such animals is very high and it's going to need
uh / a lot of ingenuity / a lot of practical development to reduce the
120 costs / to make this a commercial proposition uh in normal cattle
production / cloning has also been suggested as a way of preserving

endangered species / uh and while this may have very positive vibes in public relations terms uh this is highly likely not to be a practical way forward / one of the requirements uh to clone an animal is a supply of
125 eggs and a uh an availability of surrogate mothers to carry the cloned embryos to term / it's been suggested for example uh that uh rabbits might provide a source of eggs for cloning pandas / which would then be implanted uh in cats uh acting as surrogate mothers / uh the chance of such uh cross-species uh cloning experiments working uh
130 must be close to zero / and there must be much better ways / uh more pragmatic ways of trying to preserve the panda uh than resorting to very high-tech solutions / uh with little chance of success / even more imaginatively is the idea that you might use cloning to resurrect extinct species / here we're very much uh / in the realms of 'Jurassic
135 Park' / which I would remind uh the audience is a work of fiction / uh not uh a scientific treatise / the idea that you might resurrect the Tasmanian tiger / uh a marsupial that's been uh extinct for over 40 years / uh by taking a DNA sample from a / uh (coughs) uh DNA from a sample that's been in a bottle of alcohol uh for 150 years has been
140 mooted by one Australian museum / **this sort of project has no chance of success / uh the DNA in such material is hopelessly fragmented and the idea that you might reconstruct a complete genome from it is simply fanciful** /

In the last part of that section, shown in **bold**, how many expressions did Harry Griffin use to make clear his views on the idea of using genetic manipulation to recreate extinct species?

IELTS **TASK 5**

Section 8: Conclusion – Balancing the picture

In the final section of his talk, Harry Griffin contrasted the limited practicability of cloning with the benefit that Dolly's creation has brought. It is always important to listen carefully for the balance of a lecturer's concluding comments.

As you listen again, (circle) the positive words and expressions, and underline the negative.

given that the practical uh benefits / certainly as seen now / uh for
145 uh cloning seem to be rather uh limited / why has cloning excited the scientific community as well as the media? / well the birth of Dolly / uh was a seminal event / it demonstrated uh in uh spectacular fashion uh that the cells in our bodies / are far more versatile than we previously thought / we all start life as a single cell / as a fertilised egg / uh that
150 cell divides and multiplies as the embryo uh develops / as the embryo

uh / progresses towards a a foetus and the foetus to an animal / and that single cell becomes uh many billions of cells / of perhaps two or three hundred different cell types / and that process of gradual differentiation was presumed by developmental biologists / at least as
155 far as mammals are concerned / to be irreversible / it was a one-way process / Dolly was created from a mammary gland cell / and / uh provided uh spectacular evidence that the cells in our bodies are capable of being de-differentiated / uh of having their clock turned back / uh back to zero / and to start life all over again / the practical
160 benefits of this knowledge are uncertain / it certainly provides us with a tremendous new insight into uh our bodies / perhaps a great insight into how repair mechanisms are mobilised uh in case of human illness / and potentially has applications in new therapies based on stem cells / uh for treatment of diseases like Parkinson's uh heart attack and
165 stroke /

       so in thirty years time / _____
that cloning uh is an appropriate though limited tool to help infertile couples / or perhaps forgotten about the application at all / but hopefully we will still have / this understanding about the versatility of
170 the cells in our bodies / and it will be that / that uh Dolly will be remembered for / rather uh than all the media speculation about whether anyone is going to clone a child / and who's doing it or when / thank you /

The words missing in line 166 are important, but were said quite quickly with natural assimilation (which we looked at in Unit 2). When the teacher plays that last part of the recording again, can you identify the missing words?

Post-listening: Focus on content

Discussion and reaction

IELTS   **TASK 6**   1 In his lecture Harry Griffin contrasted the technical concerns of the scientist with the speculation of the media and 'the public at large'. Has there been much interest in cloning animals in your own country? Are people generally in favour of cloning animals, or against it? What is your own view?
2 Work with another student: one as speaker and the other as listener. Take it in turns to speak for 2 minutes, give your answers to the three points in Question 1.

3 The lecture also touched on a more controversial issue – xenotransplantation. What are the main objections to using animal organs for human patients?

4 Harry Griffin mentioned the ethical debate about the cloning of humans. Think of questions that you would have wanted to ask him at the end of his lecture. Ask them now, to provide points for your class to discuss.

Optional follow-up: Listening and note-taking
Cloning and other genetic issues are often featured in TV and radio news. Listen to a current report on one of the local English-language websites. One of the BBC websites is particularly good on these issues: http://www.bbc.co.uk/science

You could also try the website of the Roslin Institute, where Harry Griffin works: http://www.roslin.ac.uk

---

Final evaluation: Your listening and note-taking in this unit

1 Choose one of the answers below to reflect how you think you did in this unit.
   a) I was less effective than I could have been.
   b) I did as well as I can.
   c) I did better than I thought I would.

2 Compare your performance with that in the earlier units, then choose which of these phrases best describes it.
   a) I did better in this unit than in some of the others.
   b) I did less well than I did in Unit …
   c) I listened about as effectively as I did in Unit …

3 Which areas of lecture listening and note-taking do you think you need to improve most?

UNIT 7 Measuring quality of life

This unit aims to develop listening skills by:

① providing practice in the integrated use of the six macrostrategies
② providing practice in listening to a non-native lecturer
③ showing how to make use of a PowerPoint handout
④ focusing on chains of meaning
⑤ encouraging a personal listening response.

INTEGRATING THE MACROSTRATEGIES

So far we have focused on the six macrostrategies separately. In this unit and the next, we practise combining them in an effective approach to lecture listening, as shown below.

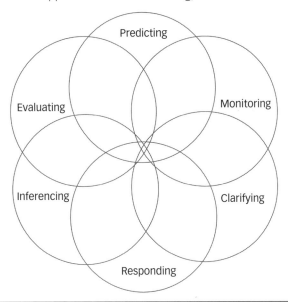

PRE-LISTENING

Introduction to the lecture topic: Measuring quality of life

In 2001, a survey was conducted in England to find out which factors people felt had the greatest effect on their quality of life. Those most frequently mentioned were:

- access to open spaces and the countryside
- crime

- education
- environmental problems and pollution
- family and friends
- health
- housing
- job
- leisure and entertainment
- money
- neighbours and the neighbourhood
- religion
- transportation.

Those factors have been listed in alphabetical order. Which factor do you think came in first place in the English survey? Which one do you think English people put in last place?

Pre-listening discussion: Content

Discuss these questions with another student.

1 Do you think the quality of your life has changed in the last five years?
2 What has contributed most to that change? Is it one of the factors in the English list, or something else?
3 Do you think that your quality of life is better than your parents' when they were your age? In what ways?

Pre-listening discussion: Language

The words shown below on the left occur in the lecture. Those on the right are definitions in jumbled order from the *Cambridge Learner's Dictionary*. Match each word with the correct definition.

1	well-being	a)	something you want to achieve in your life
2	perception	b)	position in a list which shows things in order of importance
3	index	c)	dealing with the whole of something and not
	(pl *indices* or *indexes*)		just some parts
4	holistic	d)	something you want to achieve in your life
5	ranking	e)	what you think or feel about someone or something
6	aspiration	f)	a system for comparing different values
7	ambition	g)	feeling healthy, happy and comfortable

Try to guess the meaning of the next four expressions, from their parts:

literacy rate

guesstimate

mismatch

league table

One of those four is a colloquial (informal) expression which means the same as a word in the first list on page 92. Which one?

The lecturer

The lecturer is Dr Mauricéa Lima Lynch, an economist from Recife in north-east Brazil. She worked as a university lecturer in Brazil for 8 years and then as a researcher and lecturer at Scottish and English universities for 18 years. Her main areas of interest have been labour economics and, more recently, health economics. As an academic who is at home in two languages, Dr Lynch is representative of the many international lecturers who use English as a second language to teach their academic subject.

Handout

For her lecture Dr Lynch used a PowerPoint handout, which is reproduced on pages 94–96.

The handout contains three main elements:
- an outline of the key criteria in the measurement of quality of life
- a definition and data from a UN report
- recommended further reading.

Look through it now and see whether you need to clarify any of the information before listening.

Measuring Quality of Life

Dimensions of Quality of Life

- Physical

- Mental

- Economic

- Social

UN Human Development Index Definition

"Simple summary measure of three dimensions of the human development concept: living a long and healthy life, being educated and having a decent standard of living"

(Human Development Report, 2002; p. 34)

Dimensions Measured in the UN Human Development Index

- **long and healthy life** → life expectancy at birth

- **education** → adult literacy rates combined primary, secondary and tertiary education enrolment ratios

- **standard of living** → GDP per capita

UN Human Development Report 2002 "Most Livable Countries"

1. Norway
2. Sweden
3. Canada
4. Belgium
5. Australia
6. United States
7. Iceland
8. Netherlands
9. Japan
10. Finland
11. Switzerland
12. France
13. United Kingdom
14. Denmark
15. Austria
16. Luxembourg
17. Germany
18. Ireland
19. New Zealand
20. Italy
21. Spain
22. Israel
23. Hong Kong, China
24. Greece
25. Singapore

Source: United Nations Human Development Report, 2002. New York: United Nations.

UN Human Development Report 2002 "Least Livable Countries"

1. Sierra Leone
2. Niger
3. Burundi
4. Mozambique
5. Burkin Faso
6. Ethiopia
7. Guinea-Bissau
8. Chad
9. Central African Republic
10. Mali
11. Malawi
12. Rwanda
13. Angola
14. Gambia
15. Guinea
16. Benin
17. Eritrea
18. Côte d'Ivoire
19. Congo, Dem. Rep. of
20. Senegal
21. Zambia
22. Mauritania
23. Tanzania
24. Uganda
25. Djibouti

Source: United Nations Human Development Report, 2002. New York: United Nations.

Concerns over the HDI Index

- Exclusion of important factors in determining quality of life/human development

- Differences in the quality and availability of the international data

- Meaningfulness of the index as an indicator of global human development

Useful References

- Brink S and Zeesman A (1997) Measuring Social Well-Being: An Index of Social Health for Canada. http://www.hrdc-drhc.gc.ca/sp-ps/arb-dgra/publications/research/r-97-9e.pdf

- United Nations. Human Development Report, 2002. New York: United Nations. http://www.undp.org/hdr2002

Checklist for integrating the macrostrategies

PREDICTING

Do you expect Mauricéa Lynch:
- to describe the best method of measuring life quality?
- to present alternative methods?
- to say that quality of life is simple to measure?
- to argue that it is impossible to measure quality of life?

MONITORING

Monitor your understanding of what is said and the ways in which the lecturer helps that process by:
- outlining the structure of the talk
- marking the start of new sections
- directing your attention to the information on the handout
- emphasising the contrasts between alternatives.

Monitor parts of the talk where you are less certain – then see **Clarifying** (below).

RESPONDING

As you take notes, think about your personal response to what has been said. Ask yourself:

- *Do I accept that these 'facts' are true?*
- *Do I think these views are reasonable?*
- *Do these claims match what I know?*

CLARIFYING

As you monitor the points that aren't clear, prepare questions that you would like to ask using phrases such as:

- *I didn't catch what you said about …(X)*
- *I didn't understand what you said about …(X)*
- *I don't quite see how (X) relates to (Y)*

INFERENCING

Don't expect to understand everything. Make reasonable guesses by exploiting:

- your general background knowledge
- your knowledge of the lecture topic
- the context and co-text (what has just been said)
- your knowledge of English vocabulary and grammar.

EVALUATING

Take time to assess your listening performance. Ask yourself:

- *Have I understood the main points?*
- *Have I been able to follow the argument and the examples?*

FIRST LISTENING

Listening and note-taking

TASK 1 You are going to hear the lecture played straight through, without stopping. Use the text on the left-hand side of the PowerPoint handout to guide your listening.

- Add your own notes and examples to complete the information on the handout.
- Follow the text of the definitions and quotations.
- Make a note of points you would like to get clarified.

Comparing notes and clarifying

After listening, compare your notes with someone else. Concentrate on the points you monitored as unclear.

- If there were points (or words or sections) that neither of you understood, prepare clarification questions to get the information you need.

- Ask those questions and see whether other students can clarify the points from their notes.

SECOND LISTENING

Do you think you need to listen to the lecture again to complete your notes? If not, check your notes against the sample in *Transcripts and sample notes* (pages 161–163). Then go on to *Transcript listening* (below).

If you <u>do</u> want to hear the talk again, discuss with the teacher on which areas you need to concentrate during the second listening.

Comparing notes

After listening again, compare your completed handout with the one on pages 161–163 in *Transcripts and sample notes*.

AFTER LISTENING

Post-listening: Focus on language
Troubleshooting

Are there sections of the lecture that you and the other students in your class found particularly tricky? If so, discuss what you think caused the problem, so the teacher can include further practice on them as you work through the sections of the transcript.

Transcript listening

As usual we will be working through the talk transcript in sections, using each one to highlight particular aspects of spoken language.

Section 1: Outline – definition and methods

TASK 2 As you listen to the opening section, complete the five gaps.

> good morning / what I'd like to do in this uh short talk is to discuss some of the ways uh researchers try to measure quality of life or well-being and the difficulties with such measures /
>
> one simple definition of quality of life links it to the fulfilment of
> 5 personal goals / of course the perception of high or low quality of life is subjective and may differ from individual to individual / _____ have attempted to measure quality of life / concentrating on different dimensions of life according to their particular areas of interest / _____ have tried to

10 measure quality of life by studying subjective well-being and
attempting to develop national indices of happiness / in the area
of uh _____
hundreds of different research instruments / mainly based on
questionnaires / have been developed to measure quality of life of
15 patients after medical treatment / _____
used to measure health-related quality of life / indicates
_____ that researchers have encountered in
trying to find a valid and reliable measure which can
be used in a way that is really meaningful

When you have filled in the gaps, check them against the notes you
took earlier. Are all the points included in your notes? They
represent the key points in that section.

Section 2: The many dimensions of 'quality of life'

TASK 3 Before you listen, read the transcript and try to guess the missing
words. Then listen to the section and complete the gaps.

20   quality of life of course does not _____ only
to health status but is in fact multi-dimensional / it relates to physical,
_____, economic and social well-being / when
we move from the _____ of the individual to
international comparisons of quality of life / we find that the
25 methodological _____ become even greater /

traditionally / economists have used levels of standard of living as
_____ of quality of life among countries and or
within countries / for most of the 20th century the only measurement
used to compare the standards of living of _____
30 of different countries was national income / this was often
_____ for various reasons / the main one being
that standard of living should not be analysed only in terms of
economic growth / in the second half of the 20th century economists
and other social scientists started to develop indices which
35 _____ social as well as economic indicators / the
aim of these indices was to give a more holistic picture of the living
conditions of different _____ / in this context the
terms 'quality of life', 'social well-being' and 'human development'
seem to be used _____ /

Section 3: The Human Development Index

TASK 4 This section features several examples of 'information recycling', where Mauricéa Lynch reformulated or expanded a point she had just made or a term she had just used.

As you listen, (circle) the marker expressions she used to show that she was recycling information to help her audience.

Towards the end of the section some words have been omitted. Complete the gap.

40   the best-known of these indices is the United Nations' Human Development Index / or HDI / which was first published in 1990 / and I'd like to take a few minutes to talk about this particular index / the HDI is described in the UN Human Development Report for 2002 as a 'simple summary measure of three dimensions of the human

45 development concept: living a long and healthy life, being educated and having a decent standard of living' / so there are three parts to this particular index / long and healthy life, education and standard of living / now / the concept of living a long and healthy life is captured by life expectancy at birth / although / life expectancy does measure

50 length of life it doesn't necessarily reflect health status / in other words it isn't always true that individuals who live longer are also healthy / in particular in the last years of life /

educational attainment is measured in the HDI by two indicators / by adult literacy rates that is, the proportion of people aged at least 15

55 years old who can read and write a short simple statement on their everyday life / and also by the ratio of combined enrolments in primary, secondary and tertiary education /

the final element in the HDI is standard of living and that is measured in terms of Gross Domestic Product per capita / that is GDP / divided

60 by the total population /

so how is the index calculated? / well it is calculated by averaging the values of those three dimensions of human development / life expectancy, educational attainment and standard of living / tables are then produced containing as many countries as possible / normally,

65 the number of countries uh which appear in these tables is restricted by the availability of data / although some countries with incomplete data do still appear in the tables /

the United Nations Report for 2002 gives indices for 173 countries / as you can see from the handout the Report puts Norway and Sweden at

70 the top of the list / of what are called the 'most livable countries' /
   um Canada comes third, Australia fifth and the United Kingdom
   thirteenth / of the 25 most livable countries 17 are in Europe / at the
   other end of the table the 25 least livable countries are all in Africa /
   now um _____ whether or not these rankings
75 are meaningful /

Why did Mauricéa Lynch include the expression in that gap?
   Which of the six Macrostrategies was she encouraging you to use?

Section 4: Criticisms of the HDI

In this section the focus was on the weaknesses of the HDI.
Mauricéa Lynch used a series of markers to show a chain of meaning
including these words and phrases.

criticism difficulty problem exclusion question we have to ask…

   As you listen, (circle) the markers in the transcript and underline
the weaknesses that they pointed to.

   it is widely recognised that measuring only those three dimensions
   leaves out other very important aspects of human development / and
   one of the criticisms of the UN index is that / the number of factors
   included is too limited / there are some other difficulties with the
80 index / um / I don't have time to discuss them all but I will briefly
   mention some of them / um firstly there is the problem of what the
   index is actually measuring / for example poverty is obviously a major
   contributor to poor quality of life / but the devastating consequences
   of absolute poverty are not transparent in measures like GDP per
85 capita / neither is the extent of income inequalities / another important
   exclusion is the net effect of economic growth on the environment
   and its impact on quality of life / secondly there is the issue of the
   quality and quantity of the information collected / the same
   methodology for data collection is not strictly applied in all countries /
90 and the gaps in the tables used for the calculation of the index / show
   that some components of the index are actually based on guesstimates
   / a third question we should ask is how well the Western concepts
   used in social well-being indices um reflect the way that individuals in
   non-Western cultures perceive their quality of life / this can be
95 illustrated by a discussion in Schumacher's book 'Small is Beautiful',
   when he compared modern economics / by which he meant Western
   economics / and Buddhist economics / he argued that Western
   economics measures standard of living by the amount of annual

100 consumption / assuming all the time that a person who consumes more / is better off than another who consumes less / on the other hand a Buddhist economist would see this as irrational / since consumption is merely a means to human well-being / the aim should be to obtain the maximum of well-being with the minimum of consumption / so um higher GDP per capita would not be a meaningful

105 indicator of greater human development in Buddhist economics / finally um we have to ask whether the researchers / and government officials who um develop aggregate measures of uh quality of life are really in touch with the perceptions of ordinary citizens as to what quality of life or human development is about /

Section 5: A Scottish example

IELTS

TASK 5 Mauricéa Lynch used this example to show how one group of people may not understand the needs and wants of another group in the same society. As you listen, circle the expressions she chose to refer to those two groups. Also, fill in the missing words.

110 there is an interesting example of this uh from Scotland / in 2001 a piece of research was commissioned by the government with the objective of uh understanding the aspirations of people living in Scotland / they were asked questions like / 'What are the most important changes you'd hope to see in Scotland in the next 10 years

115 in order to improve the quality of people's lives?' / 'What are the two or three most important things that should be done in order to achieve this vision of the future?' / the themes identified by the research included _____ physical and mental health / full employment and financial security / a pollution-free environment /

120 good housing, a drug-free Scotland and safety and security / the results of the research were then summarised and presented to a small group of leading decision-makers / and influential people in Scotland uh for discussion / everybody in the group except one / considered the level of ambition expressed by the public

125 _____ / although um not surprising / some of them commented um that the people had very limited ambitions / and a natural resistance to change / so / even in a country like Scotland which has a / relatively small and affluent population / those who make decisions affecting people's / quality of life / can be

130 _____ what ordinary citizens perceive as improvements in the quality of their lives / you may have examples of similar mismatches in your own country /

In one of the three gaps, Mauricéa Lynch made a slip of the tongue. What was it?

Section 6: Conclusion

TASK 6 Which expression in this final section do you think best expresses the overall point of the lecture?

> so / in conclusion / when we look at league tables of uh countries ranked according to quality of life / measured by a single figure we
135 need to be very cautious about how meaningful they are / we should uh ask ourselves whether these aggregate indices / can really represent quality of life or social well-being / of individuals with such different socio-economic, political, cultural and religious traditions and experiences /

Post-listening: Focus on content
Responding/Clarifying
If you had the chance to talk to Mauricéa Lynch about her lecture, what questions would you ask her? They could be questions to clarify what she said, or to extend what she said (or didn't say).

Discuss them in a small group and see what answers you come up with.

Responding
At two points in the lecture Mauricéa Lynch invited you to reflect on your personal response to what she had said.
1 *'No doubt you have your views as to whether these rankings are meaningful.'*
   * What is your opinion of the UN Report tables which show the most and least livable countries?
   * Do you think they are valid and reliable?
   * What purpose do they serve?
2 *'…those who make decisions affecting people's quality of life can be out of touch with what ordinary citizens perceive as improvements in the quality of their lives. You may have examples of similar mismatches in your own country.'*
   * Can you think of examples in your own country, or other countries?

Critical thinking
Can you suggest alternative ways in which governments or local authorities could improve the quality of their citizens' lives?

What changes would make the greatest difference to life quality in the city or town where you are studying?

Evaluating your performance in this unit

1 Choose one of the answers below to reflect how you think you did in this unit.

   a) I did less well than usual.

   b) I did as well as I can.

   c) I did better than I thought I would.

   d) I did better than usual.

2 Compare your performance with that in the lecture on cloning.

   a) I did better in this unit than I did in Unit 6.

   b) I did less well than I did in Unit 6.

   c) I did about as well as I did in Unit 6.

If you think you did 'less well' than on the cloning lecture, what were the main problems for you in this one?

   If you think you did better on this lecture than in the previous unit, what do you think were the reasons for that?

   Which of the Macrostrategies do you think you should focus on in the next lecture?

UNIT 8 Climate change: Evidence and action

This unit aims to develop listening skills by:

1. practising the integrated use of the macrostrategies
2. studying aspects of argument and counter-argument
3. identifying chains of reference in speech
4. showing how to notice a change of topic
5. encouraging the use of reasonable guesses
6. practising recognising a speaker's attitude from negative and positive vocabulary used
7. showing how to distinguish between descriptions of actual and potential events
8. looking at how to evaluate success in listening.

PRE-LISTENING

Introduction to the lecture topic: Climate change

Climate change is known more informally as *global warming* or the *greenhouse effect*. There is considerable argument as to whether or not the Earth's climate really is warming up. Some people have argued that any warming is due to natural variation in the global climate.

Reading

The text on the following page sets the scene for this unit's lecture by linking 'evidence' and 'action'.

1 Read it and then write three questions to ask another student:
   a) a **language** question, (about the meaning of a word or expression for example)
   b) a **comprehension** question about the content of the text
   c) an **opinion** question.

Whenever an extreme climatic event happens anywhere in the world, we now often question whether it was entirely 'natural'. Few people doubt that the climate is changing, but how certain can we be that humans are to blame, with their emissions of greenhouse gases?

The Intergovernmental Panel on Climate Change (IPCC) has been analysing the evidence for global warming for the last 12 years. It confirms in its recent Third Assessment Report not just that global warming is occurring, but that it is largely man-made, that it has begun to accelerate sharply and that it will increase far faster than previously thought.

Six years ago, its Second Assessment Report predicted that the overall warming of the planet during the 20th century would be 0.45°C. The 1990s, the warmest decade since records began in 1861, has forced the IPCC to raise its estimate of 20th century temperature rise to 0.6°C. In the northern hemisphere, the increase during the past century is likely to have been the largest of any century for the last 1,000 years.

After taking a range of factors into account, such as sunspot activity, erupting volcanoes and wind-blown dust, the IPCC concludes that: 'There is new and stronger evidence that most of the warming observed in the last 50 years is due to human activities'.

What about the future? What does the IPCC predict? According to the findings of its Report, a scenario in which fossil fuels remain the primary source of energy will bring a rise in temperature of 5.8°C over 1992 levels by the year 2100, with all its potential for catastrophic climate change. That makes it all the more critical that we take action now.

Adapted from: Peter Bunyard. 'The truth about climate change'
The *Observer* supplement on Climate Change. London, 28 October 2001.

When you have composed your three questions, ask your neighbour to answer them.

Pre-listening discussion: Content

1 Have you any direct evidence yourself that the climate in *your* country is changing?
2 Even if global warming is occurring, do you think it matters? What might the effects be? Who could be affected most?
3 What steps can governments take to reduce the effects of global warming?

Pre-listening discussion: Language

You will also hear a number of technical terms, some of which the lecturer explains or illustrates. Others, which are not explained in the lecture, are shown below.

Check them now and if any are new to you, read the definition.

a coral reef coral is a hard substance formed in the sea by small animals; it is often used as jewellery. A reef is a bank of coral close to the shore; the Great Barrier Reef, off the east coast of Australia, is the largest in the world

atolls circular coral reefs, common in the Pacific

proxy measures a proxy is something that represents or stands for something else. For example, the type of car that a person drives could be a proxy for their income level. In the lecture, 'proxy measures' are natural phenomena which indicate that the climate is changing over time

to ratify to approve (for example a treaty or agreement)

a loophole a chance to avoid doing something because of the way a law or rule has been written

the status quo the present situation

a lobbyist someone who lobbies (tries to persuade) politicians to do something, such as getting a law changed

You will also hear the lecturer refer to the World Meteorological Office and the Kyoto Protocol, which was the outcome of a UN-sponsored meeting held in Kyoto in 1997.

The lecturer

The speaker is Dr Simon Allen, director of the Centre for the Study of Environmental Change and Sustainability at the University of Edinburgh. The Centre teaches students from a wide range of countries – reflecting the global importance of the issue that he discusses in this lecture. Simon Allen is originally from London, so his accent is similar to that of Hugh Trappes-Lomax.

The way Dr Allen delivers his lecture and the language he uses provide a very good opportunity to review the various areas we have featured in the earlier units. The lecture is longer (approximately 23 minutes) than the others you have heard in this course, but you should find its overall structure clear.

In the course of his lecture Dr Allen uses about 100 words that are common across all academic fields, both in speech and in writing. To help you prepare for this longer listening and note-taking, those words have been listed on page 212. You will probably know most of them, but a few might be unfamiliar. If so, look them up in a dictionary or check the meaning with another student or the teacher.

Checklist for integrating the macrostrategies

PREDICTING

Do you expect Simon Allen:
* to say that climate change is not serious?
* to tell us about alternative methods for measuring climate change?
* to say that recent policies have been successful?
* to argue that the environment can recover?

MONITORING

Monitor your understanding of what's said and the ways in which the lecturer helps that process by:
* outlining the structure of the talk
* marking the sections
* directing our attention to the key points
* emphasizing the contrasts between alternatives.

Monitor parts where you're less certain – then see the points under **Clarifying** (below).

RESPONDING

As you take notes, think about your personal response to what has been said. Ask yourself:
* *Do I accept that these 'facts' are true?*
* *Do I think that Simon Allen's views are reasonable?*
* *Do his claims match what I know?*

CLARIFYING

As you monitor the points that aren't clear, prepare questions that you would like to ask the lecturer using phrases such as:
* *I didn't catch what you said about …(X)*
* *I didn't understand what you said about …(X)*
* *I don't quite see how (X) relates to (Y).*

INFERENCING

Don't expect to understand everything. Make reasonable guesses by exploiting:
* your general background knowledge
* your knowledge of the lecture topic
* the context and co-text (what has just been said)
* your knowledge of English vocabulary and grammar.

EVALUATING

Take time to assess your listening performance. Ask yourself:
* *Have I understood the main points?*
* *Have I been able to follow the argument and the examples?*

FIRST LISTENING

Listening and note-taking

As this is the final lecture in the course, I suggest you take notes on a blank sheet of paper. That will allow you to evaluate how well you have learnt to cope with taking notes without the support of a note-frame.

TASK 1

However, if you prefer to use a note-frame, you again have a choice of two:

- a list of content headings (page 110).
- the opening expressions from the various sections in his talk (page 111).

A third alternative is to skim the content note-frame first, to give you an overall view of what is in the lecture, and then to put it away and make notes on a blank sheet.

Remember that your aim is to make a note of the main points in the talk, but not every detail. This time you should aim to note down all the essential points *on first hearing*, rather than leaving gaps to complete on second listening.

As you listen, make use of the:

- signpost markers, including the use of direct questions
- list markers
- importance markers
- explanations of specialist terms
- examples to illustrate ideas
- strong stress on key words
- pauses indicating a new topic or section.

Climate change (CC): content headings

Intro

IPCC report

Types of evidence for CC
1 observations
    proxy measures

2 'a second line of evidence'

3

Effects of CC ...

Reasons why intern'l action is difficult
1

2

3

Ways to progress?

Conclusion

Climate change: opening expressions

I'm going to talk to you today about...

so turning to the evidence...

firstly there are observations...

but as well as these measurements...

a second line of evidence...

so the final line of evidence...

so if we accept that climate change is going to occur...

so let's just look at some of the reasons...

the second problem in getting...

and the third problem is that...

so how can we make progress...

so it's my hope that...

Comparing notes and clarifying

After listening, compare your notes with someone else. Concentrate on the points you monitored as unclear.

- If there were points (or words, or sections) that neither of you understood, compose a clarification question that will get the information you need.
- Ask those questions and see whether other students can answer them, from their notes.

Troubleshooting

Some international students have difficulty recognising an expression that Simon Allen used in the section where he was talking about the first type of evidence. Did you write one of these expressions in your notes on proxy measures?

eye scores

high scores

ice cores

ice cause

or something similar?

If there are other parts of the lecture where most people in your class had difficulty, the teacher can deal with them as you work on the relevant section of the transcript.

SECOND LISTENING (optional)

Your teacher will discuss with the class whether you need to listen again to the whole lecture, or whether to go straight on to **Transcript listening** (below).

After completing your listening, you can compare your notes with those on page 169 in *Transcripts and sample notes*.

Transcript listening
Section 1: Introduction – the size of the problem

⫶IELTS **TASK 2** Simon Allen began by stating the problem of climate change and emphasising that it is a cause for worry around the world. As you listen, write in the expressions he used in the gaps to make that point.

> I'm going to talk to you today about climate change / because I think it's one of the most serious problems that faces humanity at the beginning of the 21st century / climate change seems to be
> _____ / quite frequently in the news media we

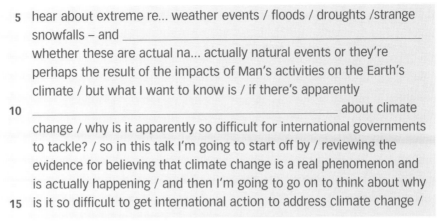

 5 hear about extreme re... weather events / floods / droughts /strange
    snowfalls – and _____
    whether these are actual na... actually natural events or they're
    perhaps the result of the impacts of Man's activities on the Earth's
    climate / but what I want to know is / if there's apparently
10 _____ about climate
    change / why is it apparently so difficult for international governments
    to tackle? / so in this talk I'm going to start off by / reviewing the
    evidence for believing that climate change is a real phenomenon and
    is actually happening / and then I'm going to go on to think about why
15 is it so difficult to get international action to address climate change /

Section 2: The IPCC report – the first type of evidence

IELTS **TASK 3** Here Simon Allen provided background details on the IPCC and
then discussed their first source of evidence. He summarised the
objection made by critics – in this case, people who do not accept
that global warming is taking place – which has to do with the *urban
heat island effect.* He then rebutted (rejected) that objection. This
pattern of argument and counter-argument is common in university
lectures.

As you listen, follow the part of the section where Simon Allen
summarised the critics' objection. He began with the words 'earlier
in previous reports', shown in **bold** in the transcript. Where did his
summary of the objection end? Mark the end with a double slash //.

Do the same at the point where he completed his rebuttal of the
objection, by marking the end with a double slash //.

    so / turning to the evidence / my comments are going to draw on
    the most recent report from the Intergovernmental Panel on Climate
    Change / this is an international panel of scientific experts that was set
    up in 1988 by the United Nations and the World Meteorological Office /
20 to advise governments on / the current state of knowledge /
    concerning the climate system / the report they made in 2001 is the
    most recent and most authoritative overview of the state of climate
    science / there are really three main types of evidence that confirm
    our belief in climate change / firstly there are observations / people
25 have measured the climate since about 1850 / the climate is of course
    interesting particularly to farmers / so / as soon as the thermometer
    was invented people started to measure temperature on a regular
    basis / these measurements of temperature show that through the
    20th century / global temperature global mean average surface
30 temperature has increased by about 0.6 degrees centigrade /

earlier in previous reports from the IPCC there was some doubt about / whether um temperature change of this magnitude had actually occurred / because people said that they were biased / there was bias in the temperature records / primarily coming from the *urban*
35 *heat island effect* / that is, that many of the temperature measuring stations are close to cities / and cities have uh have climates that are not the same as the average climate over the Earth's surface / because a great deal of energy use takes place in cities / and so / city climates are a little bit warmer than / um / than the general rural climate / so
40 some people claimed that / the apparent increase in temperature could be just due to the effect of urban… urbanisation on the temperature recording system / but in the most recent report / the global temperature dataset has been very carefully quality controlled and corrected to this effect / and there's now / um increasing confidence
45 that / a temperature change of that order has indeed occurred / but as well as these measurements it is also possible to reconstruct temperature back in time / from other so-called *proxy measures* / there are / many natural organisms that uh / they leave traces of their previous activities in the environment / that we can look at today /
50 we can measure the uh thickness of tree rings and the growth of trees is responsive to temperature and / rainfall / we can also look at the width of bandings in corals / and we can even extract information from lake sediments _____
/ so putting all the **data of this type** together it's been possible to
55 reconstruct / the changes in temperature over the whole of the last millennium / **this data** shows very clearly that the 20th century was very much warmer than the previous 900 years /
_____ **data** alone it's possible to reconstruct temperature back to 420,000 years ago / and **these data** show that /
60 the temperature now is / warmer than any time during that period

How many types of data did Simon Allen mention when talking about proxy measures?

At the end of that section, which period was he referring to when he said 'during that period'?

(Did you notice that he used the singular 'this data' and also the plural 'these data'? Both are correct.)

Section 3: The second type of evidence

:IELTS **TASK 4** Then Simon Allen turned from the topic of temperature to that of greenhouse gas levels. As you are listening, <u>underline</u> his explanations of what greenhouse gases do and why they are important.

He then referred to two things shown by the ice core evidence. What were they? (Circle) the list markers he used to highlight those two things.

> a second line of evidence is to actually look / at / the trends / in the greenhouse gases in the atmosphere / greenhouse gases are responsible for trapping heat within the Earth's atmosphere / this is a natural phenomenon / the most important greenhouse gases are water
> 65 vapour and carbon dioxide / and these have always been present in the atmosphere / they have the effect of reducing the rate at which heat is lost from Earth's surface out into space / so they keep the Earth much warmer than it would be if it didn't have an atmosphere / if it wasn't for this natural greenhouse effect / the global surface
> 70 temperature would be something like minus 15 degrees centigrade / so life as we know it could not exist / the problem is that man's activities are increasing the concentration of greenhouse gases / the most significant man-made increase is coming through carbon dioxide / carbon dioxide is emitted from any kind of activity that's based on the
> 75 combustion of fossil fuels / so any any kind of um power generation / heating / uh use of vehicles / anything that burns oil, coal or gas / causes an increase in carbon dioxide / and since the industrial revolution the um concentration has increased very rapidly / um about 31 per cent since 1750 / so again turning to the data from the ice cores
> 80 / we can see **two things** / firstly that the current carbon dioxide concentration is / clearly much higher than the concentration has been over the whole of the previous 420,000 years / also interestingly over that period the Earth's mean surface temperature has varied / and so has the carbon dioxide concentration / and there seems to be a very
> 85 tight relationship between the two / as one increases so does the other / and this gives us confidence that um / it's likely that if we change / through human activities the carbon dioxide concentration / that temperature will change / accordingly /

Section 4: The third type of evidence

IELTS

TASK 5 The final source of evidence for the IPCC report is computer modelling. As you listen and read:
- (circle) the negative words referring to the problematic nature of climate models
- underline the positive expressions dealing with the improvements in modelling
- fill in the missing words.

so the / final third / line of evidence that gives us concern about
90 climate change / is the evidence that comes from the use of climate
models / these are very complicated computer models which aim to
simulate the whole of the climate system / that is, the interactions
between / the atmospheric circulation, the oceans, the land surface
and the the ice that is present in polar regions / the Earth system is
95 very complex and not all of the processes can be represented
adequately / either because they're not very well-known or just that it
would make the models too complicated to run on current computers /
but as time's passed / the models have been refined become and
become more detailed / and / we now have more confidence in their
100 ability to predict the future accurately / partly this has come from the
fact that the models can now predict the recent changes in climate
fairly accurately / the models have been changed so that they take into
account some of the natural influences on climate / that some people
used to claim could be responsible for the apparent climate change /
105 things like the 11-year sun spot cycle which changes the output from
the sun / or the effect of aerosol in the atmosphere that comes from
volcanic eruptions like Mount Pinatubo / very small particles suspended
in the atmosphere / reflect radiation out into space and can have a
cooling effect / _____ / and
110 we can get a good match between climate model simulations and the
past / and that gives us confidence in their use to predict
the future / we can also use them as tools to quantify the natural
variability in the climate system / one of the problems / of proving that
climate change through human agency has actually occurred / is that
115 / the climate is naturally inherently very variable / and the changes
we're looking for are quite small / the mean changes are quite small
compared with that natural pattern of variability / but now with
climate models we've been able to quantify and understand the
variability / and we can see that / the changes in temperature that
120 have occurred / particularly over the last 50 years are very unlikely to
have been to have arisen through natural factors

What do you guess the verb in the gap means?

Section 5: Impacts of climate change and efforts to reduce it

IELTS

TASK 6 (Circle) all the negative words in the first 'paragraph' below.
How many factors did Simon Allen mention which will reduce the
effectiveness of the Kyoto Protocol?

so if we accept that climate change is going to occur / what does it
mean for human society? / well some of the consequences could be
quite unpleasant / uh climate change will cause sea-level rise / and
125 many low-lying coastal areas / some of which are very densely
populated / will be vulnerable to inundation / through storms and
storm surges / there could be serious effects on agriculture /
particularly in / tropical countries where the climate is already warm
and arid / and any increase in temperature and aridity will have serious
130 impacts on crop yields / there'll be impacts on natural ecosystems /
we could perhaps see serious die-back of tropical rainforests or the
loss of coral reefs / due to due to warming of the water / these are
two of the most / diverse types of ecosystems on the planet /

so there's a lot to be concerned about / and as I mentioned before /
135 one hears people talk about climate change as if it's a real phenomena
and it's going to occur / but not very much seems to be happening
internationally to address the problem / in 1997 / the world's
governments met and negotiated the / Kyoto Protocol on climate
change / and this set up um a series of targets for emission reductions
140 that governments / at least the governments of industrialised countries
/ would be obl... would be obliged to meet by 2012 / in any case / the
targets were rather weak / amounting to something like a five per
cent reduction in emissions / when most climate scientists believe
that something like a 60 per cent reduction in emissions would be
145 required to stabilise / the concentration of CO_2 in the atmosphere /
so as it stood / the agreement wasn't likely to correct the problem / it
was just a small step in the right direction / but recently the United
States of America pulled out of the agreement / and this's had a major
impact / it's likely that it will be impossible to get the agreement
150 ratified by enough countries / for it actually to come into force and for
the targets to become / legally enforceable / and the loss of the United
States from the negotiations has allowed other / sceptical countries /
to water down the provisions and / increase the size of the numerous
loopholes that already existed in the agreement / so the future doesn't
155 look too good /

Section 6: One reason why international action is problematic

IELTS   **TASK 7**   In this section Simon Allen emphasised the contrast between the two
groups involved in the 'debate in the public media'.

a) (Circle) the expressions he uses to refer to the two groups.
b) Underline the markers of contrast.

> so / let's just look at some of the reasons why it's very difficult to
> get in... international action on climate change / the first problem is
> that the science is complex / there're lots of different / well there're
> several different kinds of greenhouse gases they come from a range
> 160 of different activities / they're going to have a lot of different impacts /
> the picture is very difficult / particularly for the general public to
> understand / the debate in the public media has been clouded by
> disinformation campaigns sponsored by people comp... / primarily
> large companies who have an interest in the status quo / companies
> 165 uh like the oil giants / power generating utilities / car companies /
> they've paid um lobbyists to try to undermine the outputs of um the
> climate scientists and have caused confusion in the public mind about
> whether or not climate change is really a serious problem / the media
> hasn't helped the situation / the media likes to present any kind of
> 170 issue as a debate between conflicting interest groups / so although
> the media's provided a channel for the consensus view of climate
> scientists to be presented / it's always chosen representatives from
> lobby groups to put up against them / and the general public rarely
> realise that the climate scientists represent a consensus of / hundreds
> 175 of scientific experts / who are pretty independent-minded / whereas
> the lobbyists represent a small group of powerful companies and have
> a very particular agenda /

Section 7: Another reason

: IELTS **TASK 8** Listen for the missing words. Write them in and then guess what
they mean.

> the second problem in getting international action is that climate
> change / is primarily caused by / the burning of fossil fuels also to
> 180 some extent by land use changes caused by agriculture / the use of
> energy and agriculture are _____ /
> the development of modern economies is very closely linked with
> energy use / there's _____
> between energy use and standard measurements of economic
> 185 progress like gross domestic product / so the idea that we might have
> to / in industrialised societies move away from fossil fuels / and
> produce all the goods and services that we currently enjoy / from
> renewable energy / is a very very daunting / very difficult prospect / it
> suggests a radical restructuring of society that many people find

190 _____ / and when you consider the very
short horizon on which most governments plan for the future / in de...
democratic countries elections / perhaps only occur every five years or
something like that / it's very hard for governments to
_____ / which / may produce / reductions in
195 the quality of life / as perceived by many of their citizens / so doing
something about climate change _____ / it
threatens the most powerful countries /

TASK 9

Section 8: The third reason why action is difficult

In this section, there are two 'chains of reference' – alternative
expressions referring to the same idea or topic. One chain refers to
developed countries and the second to developing countries.

As you listen, decide whether the underlined expressions refer to
developed countries or developing countries.

Listen for the missing words and **complete the gaps**.

and the third problem is that / climate change is really / a problem
that results from the activities of the <u>rich industrialised countries</u> / but
200 the effects are primarily going to be felt by the people / mainly poor
people / who live in <u>developing countries</u> / particularly the people who
live on small island states / like the atolls in the South Pacific / where /
the land surface is nowhere more than a few metres above sea level /
and even fairly small changes in sea level / will thr... completely
205 threaten the future existence of <u>their countries</u> / or the people in
Bangladesh and Egypt who live / um in the highly populated coastal
areas / threatened by coastal flooding / or the semi-arid tropical
countries where food security is already a problem / and reductions in
rainfall and increases in temperature will bring further water scarcity
210 and problems for agriculture / these are <u>the people who're going to
suffer</u> / <u>the countries responsible</u> for the pollution / mainly are in the
northern hemisphere / where / the impacts will be less / and more
importantly / <u>the countries</u> have strong economies and will be able to
take actions necessary to adapt to the impacts of climate change / for
215 instance / reinforcing flood defences / or strengthening infrastructure
to cope with increased storm possible increased storm damage / all all
kinds of measures are more feasible _____ /
so / to do something about climate change it requires / people / who
are not going to suffer / or believe that they won't suffer very much /
220 to care about <u>people in far away places</u> that they hardly even know /
_____ /

but the developed world needs to care for future generations /
the as yet unborn who live in these countries / this is very hard to
achieve /

You should have found that one word occurred in both gaps, but
with different meanings. **Guess what it meant** in the two cases.

Section 9: Proposals for individual and collective actions

TASK 10   Finally Simon Allen suggested ways in which individuals and
governments could help reduce climate change, and speculated on
future events. In doing so he used hedging, including modal verbs
such as *might* and *could*.

As you listen to the end of the lecture, **complete the gaps**. In some
cases he was referring to the actual or current situation, and in
others to potential future action. Decide in each case whether it was
current or **future**.

225   so / _____ make progress / in dealing with
climate change? / well _____ frustrated by
what's happening on the international scene / things seem to be going
too slowly / the measures contemplated aren't strong enough / but at
least we as individuals _____ to reduce our

230   own greenhouse gas emissions / the United Kingdom for instance /
has or a target under Kyoto / to reduce its emissions by / 12.5 per cent
by 2012 / and it's imposed a stronger domestic target to reduce CO_2
emissions by 20 per cent / just about every individual living in the UK
_____ those reductions themselves / just by /

235   reducing / their own use of fossil fuel energy / by installing energy
efficiency measures in their house / even relatively cheap energy-
efficient light bulbs / by using their cars less or not at all / um just
walking or cycling or using public transport / by making sure that they
buy their electricity from people who're offering renewable energy /

240   these measures are all possible now / and if everyone took them
_____ significant impact / but in the long term
we need action internationally / and I'm not sure how this is going to
happen / but I think the governments of developed countries need to
realise that we're all in the same boat together / and / although / the

245   direct impacts _____ developed countries
could cope with / we live in a very interlinked global economy now /
and / impacts in far-away places _____ /
through reductions in availability of agricultural products / through
international flows of environmental refugees / and the events of

250 September 11 / the terrorist attacks in the USA / remind us that disaffected people in far distant parts of the world _____ to our stability and security / so _____ to avoid / or do something to reduce / what _____ disastrous impacts of climate

255 change on some developing countries /

so it's my hope that / the developed countries will realise / that it's important to help developing countries / develop their economies and base them on / non-fossil fuel intensive means of production / so that their quality of life _____ but without increasing

260 greenhouse gas emissions to dangerous levels / but the biggest challenge is that simultaneously / developed countries are going to have to / reduce their own emissions and this _____ reductions in the level of personal consumption /

AFTER LISTENING

Post-listening discussion: Focus on content

Your predictions

1 Look back to the points on page 108 which you discussed before listening. Did Simon Allen include any of the points you predicted?

2 Are there issues that he did not include that you think are important?

Responding/critical thinking

:IELTS **TASK 11** 1 Has your government introduced policies or regulations to reduce global warming or greenhouse gas emissions? Have they been effective?

2 Do you think that the individual actions Simon Allen proposed would be effective? If not, why not?

3 What other actions – by governments or individuals – could be positive and effective steps towards reducing climate change?

Your own questions

The teacher will compile a list of further questions that the students in your class think are relevant to the issues discussed in this unit. Talk about some or all of them, in a small group.

Optional follow-up: Writing

:IELTS **TASK 12** Write a short essay (250 words) in 40 minutes, summarising your views on <u>one</u> of the questions you have discussed since hearing the lecture.

If you are interested in reading further about the current situation of climate change, try the IPCC website: http://www.ipcc.ch/pub

Evaluating your performance in this unit

1 Choose one of the answers below to reflect how you think you did in this unit:
   a) I did less well than usual.
   b) I did about as well as I can.
   c) I did better than I thought I would.
   d) I did better than usual.
2 Compare your performance with that in the lecture on quality of life.
   a) I did better in this unit than I did in Unit 7.
   b) I did less well than I did in Unit 7.
   c) I did about as well as I did in Unit 7.
3 If you think you did less well than on the quality of life lecture, what were the main problems for you in this one?
4 If you think you did better on this lecture, why was that?
5 Below is a self-evaluation checklist based on the points you considered before listening (page 108). Tick YES or NO to assess your use of macrostrategies in this unit.

Checklist for your use of macrostrategies

	YES	NO
I made predictions before the lecture		
During the lecture I tried to predict what Simon Allen was going to say next		
I monitored the ways in which he outlined and marked the lecture sections		
I monitored the ways he highlighted his main point		
I showed in my notes the points where I wasn't sure what he meant		
I asked clarifying questions about those points		
I understood the answers to my clarifying questions		
I thought about whether I accepted the 'facts' Simon Allen reported		
I thought about whether I agreed with his opinions		
I guessed at the meanings of words when I could		
I evaluated my listening at the end of the lecture		
I was satisfied with my performance in listening to this lecture		

FINAL REVIEW

Ways of continuing to improve your listening

This unit aims to develop listening skills by:

1. analysing different types and sources of listening
2. considering learners' advice on practising listening to English
3. performing a critique of the suggestions offered by a teacher of English
4. reviewing what you have gained from this listening course
5. assessing on which areas of listening you need to focus.

We are nearing the end of this course, but of course you should – and will – carry on practising and improving your English listening skills. In this unit we will be discussing different ways of doing that.

PRE-LISTENING

Introduction to the lecture topic: Types of listening

In *Study Listening* we have concentrated mainly on listening to lectures, taking effective notes and discussing the lecture content. But during a university course you will need to do other sorts of listening in and around your studies. A leading expert on the teaching of listening, Michael Rost, has suggested there are four principal types of listening:

- **Appreciative listening** – for pleasure and relaxation
  Examples: listening to music, watching TV or listening to a joke
- **Informational listening** – to gain knowledge
  Examples: listening to instructions, directions or a description
- **Critical listening** – to assess the value or validity of a message
  Examples: listening to an argument or attempt to persuade
- **Empathic listening** – to understand someone's feelings or point of view
  Examples: listening to a patient; or listening to a friend talking about an emotional problem at home.

(adapted from Rost 2002: 158)

Pre-listening discussion: Content

1 In many situations we need to do more than one of those types of listening. Which one(s) do you think we have practised in *Study Listening*?

2 Students often say that they have found it useful to practise listening by watching TV, and of course that offers a wide range of programmes. Look at the list below and decide which types of programme you think are a) <u>most useful</u> and b) <u>least useful</u> for improving your listening to English. Then discuss the reasons for your choice.
   - local news
   - political discussion
   - quiz show
   - science programme
   - film (movie)
   - drama
   - cartoon
   - American comedy
   - international news
   - weather forecast

Pre-listening: Advice on listening from other students

Before you hear the final talk, have a look at the ten suggestions below, which come from international students at the University of Edinburgh. About six months after they had begun their degree course, they were asked to describe any techniques they had devised or adapted to improve their listening comprehension.

Reading

Read what the students said. <u>Underline</u> the key points in their advice.

Student 1

I noticed that I improved much more when I got a TV but I didn't take any conscious steps to practise listening.

Student 2

In lectures they give us lots of notes, especially for the MSc classes. That made it easier and the subject was very familiar to me, so I could use my knowledge to work out what the lecturers were saying. I try to read the handouts again later, to fix the new information.

Student 3

Listening to a tape and writing down exactly what you hear is very helpful. To listen very specifically and in detail means you have to pay attention to sounds which you have some problems with yourself. Seeing what the gaps are in your dictation tells you what your listening problems are.

Student 4

I listen to the news on television or radio and then try to discuss the topics with friends. This is very useful for me to know whether the news that I have heard is correct and does not give different perspectives than my understanding.

Student 5

I improve listening by meeting a lot of friends and talking to them on any topic. The best way is to make them give explanations when I don't understand something and then to tell them what I have understood from those explanations.

Student 6

I spend quite a lot of time listening to the radio, such as the news on Radio 4, which is good practice. Especially when some of the news is repeated, that helps me to confirm what I have heard.

Student 7

Watching an interesting movie or TV programme such as The Cosby Show will attract my attention to follow the story and hence practise my English by listening.

Student 8

I think it's good practice to listen to other foreign speakers talking about your field. You have to get used to their accents, in the same way as you have get used to British people's different accents. In fact, there are bigger differences between British accents than between foreigners, I think. So it's all good practice and helps you to find out more about the subject.

Student 9

Every day I listen to different radio programmes, especially to the news, and try to understand the whole context. By listening to different dialects and speeds, my English improved quite a lot.

Student 10

I have been experimenting with 'hearing' (not listening to) novels and stories on cassette, using a Walkman, just to force my mind to think in English when I am not speaking, reading or writing.

(adapted from Anderson and Lynch 1996: 26)

LISTENING

Listening and note-taking

:IELTS

TASK 1 Now listen and make notes on the short talk on listening by Tony Lynch, which is partly based on those students' suggestions. Towards the end, he refers specifically to the advice you have read from students 3, 8 and 10.

AFTER LISTENING

Post-listening discussion

Comparing notes

After hearing the talk once, compare your notes with someone else.

1 Have you noted the same number of points?
2 Do you agree on the key information for each one? You can compare your notes with those on page 172 in *Transcripts and sample notes.*

Responding

1 Do you think it would be difficult, in your present situation, to take up any of the advice from the Edinburgh students?
2 What about the suggestions from Tony Lynch?
3 Can you suggest any solution to those difficulties? Could you adapt the advice to suit your situation?
4 Do you know of other techniques that will help students to improve their listening?

Final evaluation: Your listening at the end of this course

1 What do you think this course has helped you with most?
2 What do you feel are your main remaining problem areas in listening?
3 What would help you to reduce those problems?
4 What do you think is the most important advice you can give someone who wants to improve their listening?

Listening on the Net

More and more people are able to use the Net for English language study and practice. Among the major English-language news and science websites are:

    http://www.CNN.com
    http://news.bbc.co.uk
    http://www.ABCNEWS.com
    http://www.tvnz.co.nz
    http://www.abc.net.au
    http://www.CBC.ca

For lecture listening practice, I strongly recommend the Reith Lectures. They are an annual series on BBC Radio 4 UK, given by leading academics. The topics covered in recent years have included neuroscience (2003), social accountability in government (2002), the 'greying' (ageing) of society (2001) and global development (2000).

The website for the current series is
http://www.bbc.co.uk/radio4/reith2003

The website provides background information on the topic and the lecturer. You can watch and listen to the lecture, and you also have access to a full transcript. We have found it makes excellent material for independent listening and note-taking practice.

Accent summary – Main features of the native-speaker lecturers' accents

These are the main vowel differences between the accents of the native-speaker lecturers. In each case, the shading shows the speaker(s) whose pronunciation is distinctive. The words in *italics* occur in the opening or closing section of the speaker's lecture. They are also shown tinted in the complete transcripts (pages 134–168).

vowel symbol	example word	1 Canada	2 New Zealand	3 Australia	4 S. England (RP*)
/ɑ(r)/	part	*large* *cars* *farmers* *are better*	*departments* *arts*	*car*	*partner*
/3(r)/	first	*urbanisation* *turn* *return* *first*	*tertiary* *university* *first*	*working* *learning* *first* *returning*	*first*
/e/	bet	*stem* *developing* *second*	*education* *chemistry* *sections* *essays*	*ten* *affects* *sector* *less*	*eventually* *said* *friend*
/ɑ:/	after	*example*	*ask* *arts*	*past* *advantage*	*advantages* *disadvantages*
/ʌ/	cut	*countries* *thus* *enough* *such*	*culture* *countries* *assumptions* *studying* *subjects*	*number* *someone*	*none* *result* *others* *run*
/æ/	hat	*land* *families* *adequately*	*examine* *language* *actually* *imagine*	*that's* *rapid* *naturally*	*thanks* *bad* *cat* *fact* *tact*

* Received pronunciation

5 Scotland	7 N. England	8 S. England (London)	Comments
targets *scarlet*	*started* *large*	*aren't* *target* *cars* *far*	Scots and Canadians pronounce all r sounds. Other speakers sound r only before a vowel
first *birth* *were*	*birth* *first* *maternal* *inserting*	*per cent* *term*	As above
preventive *medicine* *ten* *healthier*	*cell* *speculation* *step* *pregnant*	*energy* *measures* *help*	Speakers from New Zealand tend to pronounce this sound as /i/, so that 'bet' sounds like 'bit'
contrast *last*	*transfer* *implanted*	*transport* *disastrous*	The two southern English speakers use a long back vowel /ɑ/. The others pronounce it as /æ/ or /ʌ/
discuss *countries* *doubled* *results*	*adult* *public* *done* *pulse* *just*	*frustrated* *enough* *something* *bulbs*	In the north of England, the vowel in 'cut' is pronounced like 'foot'
back *contaminated* *that's*	*mammal* *fascination* *hasn't* *practical* *applications*	*happening* *gas* *impact* *action*	Northern English speakers pronounce this rather like the vowel in 'but'

Transcripts and sample notes

Introduction Two functions of listening

TONY LYNCH

hello / my name's Tony Lynch / um I'm the person who wrote this course / um I've been interested in listening ever since I spent three weeks in France uh when I was at secondary school / and I found that the French I heard people speaking was so very different to what we were taught at school / and that's where my interest in foreign language listening comes from /

I think that listening has two main functions for the language learner / firstly it's a route to information to content / and secondly it can be a rich source for learning about the spoken language / and both of these apply to listening to lectures /

firstly as regards listening for information there are two sorts of help that you can use / one is that on a university course the topics are going to be relatively familiar to you / so you can use your existing knowledge to help you understand what the lecturer is saying / and the second point / is that because each lecture series is part of a larger programme / you can make mental connections with what you've heard from other lecturers in the same course /

but lecture listening can also be a great source of learning about the spoken language / in our case, English / and you can use lecture listening to build up your knowledge in various areas of spoken English / firstly it applies obviously to vocabulary / and I'm thinking here not so much about technical terms / which I would put on the content side of the lecture / I'm thinking / more of the informal words you hear in speech / uh words like 'snags' instead of 'problems' / another one would be 'in a nutshell' / instead of 'in brief' / uh then there are also differences between spoken and written grammar / for example

lecturers tend to say / 'I'm going to talk about so-and-so' or 'what I'm going to talk about today is so-and-so' / whereas if they were writing they'd probably use 'will' / 'this paper will focus on …' or the present simple / 'this article focuses on…' / and then a third aspect which is crucial in lectures is the practice you get in listening to natural pronunciation / just now I gave you the example of 'going to' / now in fact a lecturer will probably not pronounce it as 'I'm going to' / they're more likely to say 'I'm gonna' or they may even reduce that to 'angna' / now mentally translating 'angna' into 'I am going to' is something you have to get used to / in lectures /

so those are the two key functions of listening / and in *Study Listening* we're gonna focus on both of them / we'll be discussing the information content of what the lecturers have said / and we'll also be studying the forms of spoken language that are common in lectures /

LISTENING : TWO main functions
  ① route to info/content
  ② source for learning abt spoken lang.
  both true for list'ing to lectures

① Listening for info.
  Two sorts of help:
       1. existing world knowledge

       2. mental connections with other lectures

② Listening as source for L'ing abt spoken lang.

    1. vocab: probs not tech. terms, but informal words
         "snags" = problems
         "in a nutshell" = in brief
    2. grammar differences
         spoken Eng : "going to"
         written "   " will" or Pres. simple
    3. Natural pronunciation
         I'm going to → "gonna" → "angna"

STUDY LISTENING focuses on both info. and
                       language sides of learning

Unit 1 Problems of urbanisation

ADRIENNE HUNTER

today **I want to discuss** problems of urbanisation / in particular **I want to talk about** those problems which are peculiar to developing economies / and **to discuss** three possible policies / which could be used to control or uh / to stem / uncontrolled urbanisation in developing countries /

certain urban problems of course are common to both developed / and developing countries / for example / poor housing, unemployment, problems connected with traffic / for example air pollution, congestion and so on / however there there are problems which are very peculiar to developing economies / and this is due to the fact that developing countries need to create a basic infrastructure / which is necessary for industrialisation / and consequently for economic growth / in fact it's the provision of this infrastructure which constitutes the urbanisation process itself / and this uh infrastructure / or rather the / provision of this infrastructure / may have undesired effects on the economy as a whole / **now it's these undesirable consequences of … or effects which I'd like to deal with first** /

I'm going to talk about five main consequences of this uncontrolled urbanisation _//_ in the first instance there's the problem of the migration of people from the country to the city / people living in the country often see the city as a more desirable place to live / whether they're living in developing or developed countries / but the problem is much more serious in a developing country / because there are in fact more people who wish to migrate to the city / now the fact of people migrating to the city causes a certain depopulation of rural areas _//_ and a second consequence / is the result / or the result of this is a decrease in the production of food / and in the supply of food to the country as a whole / this in turn can also lead to a rise in prices / because of the law of supply and demand _//_ as a result of people moving to the city / you get a high urban population growth rate / now this isn't not this isn't due not only to the fact of more adults moving to the city / but can also be due to traditions of these people from the country / who perhaps from rural areas have a tradition of large families and so on / so the ci… population of the cities increases with these numerous children of large families _//_ this leads to a fourth consequence / which is a dramatic pressure on the supply of social services in urban areas / in particular / services related to health and education / in relation / in relation to health services / we can see that there are endemic diseases which could be made worse by overcrowding / people coming from the country to the city / and for example in the stresses on services in education / with more children there's a need for more schools and more teachers and so on and so on _//_ a fifth area which is affected by uncontrolled urbanisation is that of the labour supply / often uncontrolled urbanisation leads to an excess of labour supply in the cities / and this can lead in turn to an informal kind of labour activity / which might be called low-prod… productivity activities / for example people selling things in the streets / or for example you often find in large urban areas in a developing country / **children who watch cars** while their owners are doing something else / and then they **ask for tips** when the owners return / this is really a sort of undesirable type of labour / so these are in fact the main consequences of uncontrolled urbanisation /

now I'd like to move on to three **possible** policies which **could be** developed / to stem this kind of uncontrolled urbanisation in developing countries / the first one **would be** to promote a more equal land distribution / in this way farmers **would be** more motivated to stay on the land / they **would be** able to work more land and thus be able to feed their families more adequately / often the reason why farmers wish to go to the city is that they cannot grow enough food to both feed their families and earn a living / so a more equal land distribution is one such policy to stem this kind of move to the city / a second policy **would be** to improve the supply of social services in the rural areas / particularly in the field of health and education / country people often f… move to the city because they feel that these services are better in the city / if they **could compare** the services they they receive which are improved and the ones in the city they **might feel** there was **perhaps** not much difference / and it **would be** another reason for not moving / a third **possible** policy **would be** to give financial assistance to agriculture / especially to the small landowner / now obviously the problem of uncontrolled urbanisation / and the consequences which are not favourable / is a difficult problem / to resolve / but these three types of policies **could help** to reduce the problem / which is felt in particular in developing countries /

Probs of urbanis'n

Intro	some prob's common to dev'd + dev'ing countries (e.g. traffic)
	others specif. to dev'ing, due to need for infrastructure
	(provision of infrastr = urbanis'n)

Consequences/eff's	5 consequences of uncontrolled urbanis'n:
	1. migration to city
	2. depop'n of rural areas: fall of food prod'n, so rise in prices
	3. high urban pop. growth rate because more adults in city + rural trad'ns of large families
	4. pressure on social services
	5. increase in lab. supply leads to low-paid activities (e.g. street vending, car watching)

Policies	3 poss. policies
	1. more equal land distrib'n, so farmers will stay on land because able to feed families
	2. improve rural soc. services
	3. financ. aid to agric. (esp. small landowners)

NB **no easy solution**, but policies could help

Unit 2 Differences between academic cultures

OLWYN ALEXANDER

hello / my name's Olwyn Alexander / I teach at a university in the United Kingdom / and I help / overseas students to improve their academic writing skills / I often ask the students to reflect on the differences in education culture between the system in their countries and the UK / I think this helps them to critically examine some of the assumptions they make about uni… about writing at university / today I'm going to share with you my own reflections about differences in education culture / and **I'm going to tell you a story** which I hope will show you what I mean by education culture / and how important it is to be aware that differences exist when you move from one education culture to another /

the two cultures I'm going to talk about will seem on the face of it to be very similar / they are New Zealand and the United Kingdom / New Zealand was a colony of the UK / so English is the main language in both countries / and the New Zealand education system is based on the British one / it has primary secondary and tertiary level education / with the tertiary **or university** level organised around departments / grouped into schools / **or faculties** / actually I've got experience of studying in several faculties / science and arts in my first degree / and social science much later on / in my postgraduate study / my first degree was in chemistry and physics / but it was modular / and I was able to take up to five modules outside the School of Science / I chose to study English literature / in the School of Arts and Humanities / I don't suppose you could imagine / two more different subjects / **but I'd always been unable to decide** between science and arts and this was an opportunity to keep going with both of them / as you can imagine / there are a lot of differences in the way that science and arts students write / and what they have to write about / sciences focus on activity-based skills such as describing procedures, defining and solving problems / the arts are more interested in seeing that students can analyse several sources / from different authors / and synthesise these into their writing / science undergraduates write reports / with well-defined sections and subsections / with headings / and arts undergraduates write essays /

my story concerns that little word *essay* / and my understanding / **or rather / my misunderstanding of it** / in the two education cultures I'm going to talk about / first I just need to tell you a little bit about these two cultures / they were both called social science / some years ago I studied for a Masters degree in Applied Linguistics / here in the UK / in order to understand more about English and learn how to teach it more effectively / several years before I'd begun to study a postgraduate diploma in teaching English as a foreign language / in New Zealand / but as it happened I was not able to complete that diploma / now the content of these courses was very similar / they had the same kinds of modules and the same **or very similar** reading lists / however as I discovered / the writing tasks were quite a bit different / and the view of what constituted a successful outcome was also / quite different /

to get back to that little word *essay* / you might like to think for a moment what an essay is / how would you write if you were asked to write an essay? / for me an essay's a logically connected piece of prose / which sets out to make a number of points in order to answer a question / this question's usually posed in the introduction and answered in the conclusion, on the basis of evidence drawn from the points made in between / **or so I thought** / I'd written a number of essays for my TEFL diploma course / and got rather good marks / but pride comes before a fall / on the Applied Linguistics course the first writing task was an essay / just to see if we knew how to write one / 'no problem' I thought / 'I know what one of those is' / I struggled a little with the writing, as I do with all writing tasks / even though I think I am quite an experienced writer / but what I produced I thought was a reasonable attempt at an essay / however I got quite a low mark for it / and I went to my tutor to find out why / **'well' he said** / 'what you wrote was quite different from all the other students' / 'in what way?' / **I asked** / 'well it was like an undergraduate essay' / an undergraduate essay? / I was a bit cross / 'undergraduate? / Alexander Pope wrote essays / Charles Ra… Lamb wrote essays / were these undergraduate too?' / you can see I had quite a good opinion of my ability to write at this time / 'what did the other students do?' **I asked** / 'well theirs were postgraduate projects with sections and subsections / with headings' / 'oh' says I / just a little ironically / 'you want me to make it look like a scientific report?' / 'well yes' / **the tutor said** / I discovered later in my course that social science in the UK / and possibly also in New Zealand **I just hadn't been aware of that fact** / was suffering from what was called *physics envy* / **or the desire to look scientific** / researchers in the so-called soft sciences envied the hard sciences for their ability to run experiments / control variables / and produce reliable data / and they attempt to introduce the scientific method into their research / and report it in scientific ways / hence the style of the essay I had to write / which should really have been called a *project* all along /

of course the contrast is not nearly as simple as I'm making out / but I don't really have time to go into that today / but this was my first lesson that different education cultures had different ideas about ways to communicate within their cultures / even though on the face of it they seemed as if they should be very similar / I learned a number of things from this, I think / **first of all / I learned that** the dictionary definition of a word / **or the assumptions you've built up about it** / may not necessarily be very useful when you move to a new education culture / **then I learned** the necessity of paying attention to your audience / and finding out about their assumptions / particularly if they're going to grade your work / **and I also learned** that it's essential for me to teach my writing class students / how to research the academic cultures they'll be studying in / and pay attention to the way that culture chooses to communicate its knowledge / and its research results / there'll be differences related to the level of study / undergraduate **or postgraduate** / the particular discipline / sciences **or social sciences** / and even the particular subject and department that the course is taking place in / **so we cannot generalise** across the whole of academic / um / education and find **one essay or report that fits all** /

Differences between academic cultures

Outline:

    1 thoughts on diff's in ed culture

    2 story to show what ed culture is + diffs

two cultures   NZ + UK
NZ ex-colony, ed system based on UK – prim, sec + tertiary
univ . faculties/schools . departments

OA's experience
Sciences + Arts for 1st degree (chem, phys, but Eng Lit)
Social Science for PG degree

diff's between Sciences and Arts
Sciences / activity-based skills (describing, defining, solving problems)
Arts / Ss have to analyse several sources and synthesise in own writing

Sciences UGs write reports (sections, subsections)
Arts UGs write essays

OA's story – 'essay'
she did Masters in Applied Linguistics in UK
had done Dip in Teaching EFL in NZ
similar courses but writing tasks different

when OA did 'essay' for UK Masters course, got low mark
went to see tutor, who said she'd written an UG essay
OA asked what problem was
tutor said she hadn't used sections, subsections and headings
she'd written a NZ 'essay'
the UK 'essay' would have been called 'report' or 'project' in NZ

The lesson
that diff. ed. cultures have diff. ideas about communication
1 dictionary meanings of a word may not help
2 need to pay attention to your audience when writing
3 can't generalise across different acad. disciplines

Unit 3 Teleworking and distance learning

RON HOWARD

teleworking literally means working at a distance / that is, far from the office or normal place of work / usually though not always this means working at home / but that's not to say that everyone who works at home is a teleworker / teleworking / also called *e-working* or *telecommuting* / has come to mean specifically working at home but communicating with the office by telephone or computer link / related to teleworking is distance learning or *telestudying* as it can also be called / and much of what I have to say about teleworking also applies to distance learning and teaching /

there's been a rapid increase in the number of teleworkers and telestudents over the past ten years or so / naturally this growth in the number of teleworkers affects only certain occupations / workers involved include those in the information sector especially / but also business professionals and scientists / and also teachers / in some cases people are being persuaded or even forced to become telecommuters / but often they choose to do so themselves / why do people choose to work at home? / well there are a number of advantages for the worker / and also for the people who employ them / and for society in general / let's look at these /

first of all what are the advantages for the worker? / I would say the main advantage is that less time is spent commuting / that is travelling to and from work / someone working in a big city like London can easily spend an hour or more travelling to work / and the same amount of time returning home / two or three hours a day can therefore be saved / and this is time that can be spent in more profitable ways than sitting in a train or

car / commuting is quite stressful / and teleworking eliminates that stress / not having to travel saves not only time but also money / bus or train fares can amount to hundreds of pounds a year / motoring costs are also high / working at home can be more convenient than working in an office / work time can be scheduled to suit the worker rather than the boss / breaks can be taken as and when needed rather than according to fixed schedules / and it's generally pleasanter working in the comfort of your own home / there's no need to dress up and so on / the choice of a place to live no longer depends on nearness to the office / less expensive and more attractive areas far from the city now become a possibility / finally people who can't leave home for any reason can work as telecommuters / for example those with disabilities / or the need to look after small children or elderly parents /

recent surveys have shown that 68% of people who telecommute want to continue / but / 32% want to return to central office working / why? what are the disadvantages? for one thing the worker may have to equip his home at his own expense / this means buying a computer and peripherals such as a printer and perhaps also a fax machine / heating and lighting bills are likely to be higher / and there's also the question of insurance / these costs have to be set off against the savings from not having to travel / even if the employer pays for the equipment / home working makes a demand on space / a spare bedroom may have to be converted into an office /

more importantly perhaps someone working at home will not have the backup that can be taken for granted in an office / technical staff to troubleshoot computer problems will not be on hand for example / there's also a loss of social support from co-workers / there may be many distractions in the home / from a partner or from young children / there'll be many temptations to put off work in favour of more agreeable alternatives or even of domestic chores / the teleworker needs to be highly motivated / or at least extremely self-disciplined / many teleworkers are self-employed or part-time workers, and so they don't have the advantages of full-time employees / for example paid leave, accident and sickness cover / they may also need / they may also be paid less / in other words they're in danger of being exploited by less scrupulous employers keen to take advantage of the situation /

so what are the advantages and disadvantages for the employer? / the major advantage for the employer is saving on costs / the employer doesn't need to provide workspace and equipment / there are savings in running costs such as rates, electricity, catering / and telecommuters in some cases receive lower payment for their work /

surveys seem to show that teleworkers are more productive than their counterparts / one study suggests that they're 20–45% more efficient / so for a smaller outlay of money an employer can obtain more product and therefore greater profits /

on the other hand, the employer can't easily supervise what the workers are doing / he or she may feel it necessary to visit the workers at home on a regular basis / this involves time and money / an additional issue in these home visits is that workers may resent what they see as intrusion into their personal lives /

converting to teleworking obviously requires a great deal of reorganisation / lack of experience in the field means that the employer will either need to engage an expert to help in the reorganisation / or risk making costly mistakes /

the move to teleworking has implications for society as a whole / if workers no longer need to commute there'll be less traffic on the roads and therefore fewer accidents and less pollution / since the disabled and others can now work as telecommuters there may be a reduction in unemployment / and if workers are more satisfied society as a whole will be happier / with the poss… with possible reductions in illness and crime /

again there are possible disadvantages / with many people working at home there may be greater consumption of electricity, gas / finally, as I've already pointed out / teleworking is not possible in many occupations / building workers, street cleaners, shop assistants and many others will have to continue to work outside the home / and this may lead to dissatisfaction and resentment /

let's now consider briefly distance learning / in many ways it's parallel to teleworking with the same advantages and disadvantages / convenience is again the main advantage for the learner / especially for those who live in remote areas / for example in the outback of Australia or the Highlands and Islands of Scotland / it also benefits those who cannot easily attend a university or college for other reasons / such as disability / telestudying also allows people to choose a course which isn't available locally / people with a full-time job can combine work with study by doing a distance learning course / this has obvious economic benefits / in addition a distance learning course may be cheaper than a conventional one / as with teleworkers, distance students can please themselves when to do coursework and are not forced to study at fixed times /

one disadvantage is that a distance learning course usually takes longer to complete than a face-to-face course / this may lead to loss of motivation and 'drop-out' / or failure to finish the course / as with teleworking distractions in the home may be a problem / it can be difficult to find the quietness needed for study away from children or flatmates / television, music, conversation are all too easily available / telestudents need to be at least as highly motivated as teleworkers /

perhaps even more so than work / learning is dependent on other people / both tutors and fellow students / feedback from tutors is essential / and tends to work best if immediate rather than delayed / students learn from each other / not only from books and teachers / so the lack of support from tutors and students is important / so is the lack of library and other facilities /

finally some subjects are less suitable for home study / languages for example / learning to communicate / which after all is the principal aim for most language students / demands the presence of others /

if tutors on distance courses work at home they benefit in the same ways as teleworkers in general / even if they work in an office they'll still enjoy some of the flexibility of home working / at the same time / tutors have a managerial role / and just as managers in business / may find it difficult to supervise employees adequately / distance course organisers have to take particular care with accreditation / the absence of face-to-face contact interferes with the giving and receiving of feedback / which is so vital to teaching and learning / printed materials need to be specially written to try to overcome this loss / although such technological aids as audio- and videoconferencing can help / it's arguable that nothing can replace a good teacher in a classroom /

so to sum up / many of the advantages have corresponding disadvantages and vice versa / but the drawbacks can often be overcome by careful planning / the balance of advantages and disadvantages will obviously depend on the individuals and the situations concerned / teleworking and telestudying will never completely replace conventional work and study practices / both types of work and study have their place / perhaps the ideal is to combine the two / working or studying at home / but with regular visits to the office or classroom /

These notes are based on Ron Howard's own speaking notes:

Advantages	Disadvantages

WORKER

savings in time and money (no commuting)	cost of equipment and overheads
	space needed for work
less stress	lack of technical backup + contact with co-workers
flexible working hours	
greater comfort and convenience	domestic distractions
greater choice in place to live	need for self-discipline
those unable to travel can work	loss of benefits of full-time employment

EMPLOYER

cost savings	loss of supervision
greater productivity	time and money for home visits
	reorganisation necessary

SOCIETY

less pollution from cars	greater consumption
fewer accidents	dissatisfaction and resentment
less unemployment	
happier citizens	
less crime and sickness	

LEARNER

convenience	longer completion time
availability	distractions
flexibility	lack of support
economic benefits	lack of facilities
	more suited to some subjects

TUTOR/COURSE ORGANISER

flexibility	care needed with accreditation
	absence of face-to-face contact
	materials must be specially written
	nothing can replace good T in classroom?

Conclusion
- Balance of pros and cons depends on indiv. + situation
- TW and DL won't replace conventional work and study
- Ideal – <u>combine</u> the two?

Unit 4 Language strategies for awkward situations

HUGH TRAPPES-LOMAX

some time ago I was in a bicycle shop / looking for a new lock for my bicycle / the shopkeeper / showed me several / patiently explaining their advantages and disadvantages / none of them was quite what I wanted and eventually I said to the shopkeeper / 'I'll think about it / thanks very much' / and left the shop / why did I say 'I'll think about it'? / not something more straightforward like / 'none of these is right' / 'they're too big' / 'they're too small' / 'they're too expensive' / 'I'll go elsewhere' /

I think there are two reasons why I chose to say 'I'll think about it' / the first is I didn't want the shopkeeper to feel that his products were not valued or that his time had been wasted / second / is that I didn't want to be the object of his possible annoyance or irritation / in other words / I didn't want him to feel bad / and I didn't want me to feel bad /

we have words for this general behaviour pattern of not wanting ourselves or other people to feel bad as a result of / the interactions that we have have with other people / we talk about tact / which is defined in the Collins Concise Dictionary as 'the sense of what is fitting and considerate in dealing with others so as to avoid causing offence' / or we might equally call this / as many people do / *politeness behaviour* / now notice that the definition of tact talks about avoiding giving offence / it is not talking about something positive that we do in order to make people feel better than they otherwise would / so here **we are not talking about** the kind of behaviour we / get into when for example we console a friend whose cat has just been run over / or compliment our partner on a very well-cooked meal / **we are not trying here to** positively make people feel better / but trying /

to / avoid them feeling bad / so this is a negative kind of behaviour that I'm talking about / but the fact that it's negative **doesn't mean that it's not** terribly important / it is / extremely important / it is essential / to our self-preservation and to social cohesion / and for this reason avoidance behaviour is of great interest to / many different kinds of scholars / for example it's of interest to / biologists / uh who study avoidance behaviour as part of an animal's behaviour patterns / of aggression and defence / for example / uh patterns of fleeing or freezing / or producing various protective responses / we all know that when we walk through / uh Trafalgar Square the pigeons automatically fly away as our feet approach them / um we've all seen puppies who roll over on their backs and wave their tails between their legs / um when a larger dog comes along and takes an interest in them / uh some of us may have seen what a centipede does when you touch it / it rolls up in a tight coil / thereby protecting itself from possible harm / now human beings do the same kind of thing but they do it in a more / sophisticated uh way probably / and for this reason sociologists, psychologists and social psychologists uh take a great interest in avoidance behaviour / they see it as part of the means we use for maintaining good social relationships and our own and others' face / *face* has been defined as 'a person's sense of self, of public self-image' / linguists too take an interest in this kind of behaviour / because they're interested in the communication tactics and the language forms employed to avoid conflict / and maintain face / it has been said / by the linguist Jenny Thomas / that 'simply by speaking we trespass on another's space' / so linguists are interested in what language means we use to mitigate the effects of this trespassing / the essence of linguistic tact is the choice of ways of speaking which minimise unpleasantness, embarrassment or conflict /

the range of avoidance strategies can be summed up in three military metaphors /

first metaphor / is *retreat* / under this strategy we avoid meeting the person we keep away or we remain silent / or we avoid the subject or change the subject / we talk about something else /

second metaphor is the *smoke-screen* metaphor / now under this strategy what we do is use for example conventional politeness formulae such as 'excuse me', 'would you mind?', 'sorry to bother you' / or we go in for a lot of vagueness and ambiguity / we try to be imprecise / teenagers are very good at this when parents ask them questions / 'who was that on the phone?' I ask and my teenage son replies / 'a friend' / 'where are you going?' I ask / and he replies / 'out' / of course he could say a lot more but he chooses not to / he is avoiding saying things which he thinks might cause trouble / and of course we all make use of a variety of vague expressions which come readily to hand as we speak / uh 'sort of' / 'like' / 'lots of' / 'kind of' / and 'stuff' / words of that sort / I have just used one / and of course one of the things we do try to avoid when we are speaking to people is saying 'no' / uh 'no' is what sociologists call a *dispreferred response* in most contexts / and so we try to avoid it / instead of saying no / we say 'hmm yes and no' or 'that depends' or 'I suppose so' or 'up to a point' /

third and last strategy is / the *camouflage* strategy / in this strategy we choose nice words **rather than nasty** ones / kind words **rather than brutally** honest ones / this is what we call *euphemism* / defined in the Shorter Oxford English Dictionary as 'a figure by which / a less distasteful word or expression is substituted for one more exactly descriptive of what is intended' / the linguist Deborah Cameron has a shorter and uh more / striking uh description of euphemism / she simply calls it *verbal hygiene* / it's a way of keeping ourselves linguistically clean /

there are various kinds of uh euphemism / um the example we started with is a euphemism / 'I'll think about it' / but it's a euphemistic utterance **rather than a euphemistic word or phrase** / we all have a repertoire of such utterances to summon into use / when circumstances demand / 'you must come around one of these days' / we say or we hear / and this of course is not to be mistaken for a serious invitation / 'that'd be really nice' we reply or they reply / and this of course is not to be mistaken for an enthusiastic acceptance / but most euphemisms are single words or short phrases which describe / people or things in a way which disguises / or camouflages things about them which make us feel uncomfortable or uneasy / here are a few quick examples / from a number of different domains /

one familiar category is expressions which make commercial products or public services less bad than they really / seem less bad than they really are / for examp... uh for example second class on British trains is called 'standard class' / sounds much better doesn't it? / economy class on planes is called 'tourist class' / second-hand cars have been described as 'pre-enjoyed' / an old house in an advertisement may be called a 'period house' / a very small one may be called 'cosy' / a price increase is called a 'price adjustment' / all of these are clear examples of euphemistic language /

another area is the work area / in which the boss may be called the 'team leader' / or employees may be called 'human resources' / or to sack somebody is described as 'letting them go' /

a third and very large category is to do with the body and its functions / the physical part of human nature / so / the toilet for example is referred to as the 'bathroom' or the 'powder room' / having sex is referred to as 'sleeping with' somebody or 'going to bed with' them / being old is described as 'getting on a bit' or 'being a senior citizen' / dying / is called 'passing away' or humorously / 'pushing up the daisies' /

all these examples may seem amusing or even interesting / 'interesting' is itself a / uh a euphemism in some contexts by the way / uh but hardly perhaps of great social significance / recently however euphemism has come out of the private domain of interpersonal communication / and moved into the public domain / it has become political / so the last category that I want to mention I think is a very important category / it's one which is must… much discussed in the media / and it is what is sometimes called politically correct language / the term *political correctness* is almost the opposite of a euphemism because it has become associated with absurdity and excess / so for example we have joke politically correct expressions such as 'chronologically challenged' which is supposed to mean old / or 'follically different' which is supposed to mean bald / these are absurd but the main idea behind this kind of linguistic behaviour is surely a good one / at least in intention / that groups of people should be made to feel socially included **rather than excluded** and valued **rather than disparaged** / politically correct language / revolves around issues of race, of sexual orientation and of disability particularly / uh let me take one particular example to do with children / children with physical or mental problems may be called 'exceptional children' / children with mental impairments are described as 'having learning difficulties' / children in general are often these days not called 'children' / which may seem to imply exclusion from the adult world of rights and independence / but they're called 'young people' or 'youngsters' or informally 'kids' /

does all this **MATTER?** / **YES** / we **NEED** euphemisms / the **LEXICOGRAPHER** Robert **Burchfield** says 'a language **WITHOUT** euphemisms would be a **DEFECTIVE** instrument of **COMMUNICATION**' / we **NEED** them but we also need to **UNDERSTAND** them and **WATCH** them **CAREFULLY** / we need to make **SURE** / especially in the **POLITICAL** domain / that **WE** are the masters of **THEM** / not **THEM** of **US** /

COMPLETED HANDOUT
Language strategies for awkward situations

"I'll think about it"

Why say "I'll think about it"?
Reasons: **1. didn't want shopkeeper to feel product wasn't valued**
2. didn't want to be the object of annoyance

tact 'a sense of what is fitting and considerate in dealing with others so as to avoid causing
offence'   (Collins Concise Dictionary)

avoidance behaviour
e.g. **fleeing (pigeons), freezing or protective response (puppies, centipedes)**

face 'a person's sense of self, of public self-image'

'simply by speaking we trespass on another's space' (Jenny Thomas)

avoidance strategies:

three military metaphors

1 _retreat_   silence, **talk about something else**

2 _smoke screen_   polite formulae **excuse me, would you mind, I'm sorry to bother you**

ambiguity   **teenagers' replies to parents**

vague expressions   **sort of, like, stuff**

avoid "no"   **hmm yes and no, that depends, I suppose so**

3 _camouflage_   nice words

euphemism 'a figure by which a less distasteful word or expression is substituted for one
more exactly descriptive of what is intended' (Shorter Oxford Dictionary)

'verbal hygiene' (Deborah Cameron)

Examples of euphemism

products or services

second class on trains	=	**standard class**
economy class on planes	=	**tourist class**
second-hand cars	=	**pre-enjoyed**
old house	=	**period house**
very small	=	**cosy**
price increase	=	**price adjustment**

work

boss	=	**team leader**
employees	=	**human resources**
to sack someone	=	**to let them go**

body and its functions

toilet	=	**bathroom, powder room**
have sex with	=	**sleep with, go to bed with**
being old	=	**getting on a bit**
die	=	**pass away, push up the daisies**

political correctness

"chronologically challenged"	=	**old**
"follically different"	=	**bald**
(AIM?)		**to make people feel socially included**

children

with physical /mental problems	=	**exceptional children**
with mental impairments	=	**having learning difficulties**
generally, not "children", but	=	**young people, youngsters, kids**

Conclusion: Does this matter?
Yes, we need euphemisms. But need to watch them carefully.

Unit 5 Targets for preventive medicine

ERIC GLENDINNING

well / good morning everybody / **I'd like to talk to you today** about the role of preventive medicine / **first of all I'm going to discuss** changes that have been brought about in our own society / and **then discuss** some of the problems that remain for preventive medicine to tackle / **finally** / if there's time / **I'd like to contrast** the the targets of preventive medicine in our own society / with the goals of preventive medicine in developing countries /

if we look back a hundred years ago / in the United Kingdom / four out of ten children died in childhood / those who survived birth / uh in the first few months of life were faced with diseases such as diphtheria, whooping cough, scarlet fever and tuberculosis / in the city slums the lower classes of society suffered from nutritional deficiencies / the deformities of rickets were quite prevalent / and all classes of society were vulnerable to water-borne infections / such as enteric fever / that is, typhoid and paratyphoid / and cholera / from water supplies contaminated by sewage / today the population of the United Kingdom has doubled / and that's in spite of a fall of 50% in the birth rate / and only a very small minority of families suffer the loss of a child / now / that we are **healthier** today and that we live **longer** is not the result of **curative** medicine / but of **preventive** medicine / I don't want to discount the important developments in curative medicine over the last sixty-odd years or so / forexamplethedevelopmentofuhsulphonamides / andtheantibioticsespeciallypenicillin / but the success / the success story is really one which results from preventive medicine /

let's look at some of the factors in this story /

immunisation against diphtheria, tetanus, whooping cough and polio in the first year of life protects the child from these diseases / the provision of infant clinics / health visitors / together with improved nursing standards and midwifery standards / have helped reduce infant mortality / screening measures / you'reprobablymostfamiliarwithmassradiography / the screening for tuberculosis / screening measures help detect diseases in their early stages / before they've reached a dangerous stage / we can add to those preventive measures something which I'll put under the term '**the sanitary revolution**' / if you think of the industrial revolution as being what created the wealth of this country / the sanitary revolution created the healthy society that we have today / the sanitary revolution I suppose really dates from the Public Health Act of 1875 / which resulted in **piped water supplies** / although ironically one of the first attempts at improving the water supply in this country helped increase the incidence of cholera / the introduction of the flushing toilet in London increased the quantity of raw sewage entering the Thames / and the pumping stations for London's water supply were heavily contaminated as a result / not only piped water supplies were important / but provision of **cheap soap** / people began to wash more frequently / **public bath-houses** were built and **wash-houses** / people started to wear **cotton underclothes** instead of wool / and cotton is more easily washed / more likely to be washed more more frequently / people enjoyed a **better diet** / due to such diverse factors as **the refrigerated ships bringing in** South American beef / New Zealand lamb / and so on / making available to all classes of society fresh fruit and cheap and fresh meat all the year round / **birth control** / the fact that children are now spaced out so that homes are no longer so crowded / uh as they were / no longer so overcrowded / so that the factors which lead / which allow tuberculosis to flourish have been controlled / in the workplace Factory Acts have made **working conditions** much better / so that we're no longer subjected to the same industrial diseases which were prevalent in Victorian times /

well having discussed the success of preventive measures in the past I'd like to look now at the problems which remain for preventive medicine to tackle / and you'll note that these are no longer problems due to our external environment /*althoughwecan'tdiscounttheproblemssuchasthechemicalpollutionofourfoodandtheair* / but most of the problems which preventive medicine has to tackle today are the result of our own behaviour / now let me list some of these problems for you they're on your handout / the first one is drug abuse / and I'm interested here / I'm concerned with the two main drugs / alcohol and tobacco / alcohol is a contributing factor in many road accidents *somethinglikeathirdofallfatalroadaccidents* / in a third of these cases the driver / or one of the drivers involved / has alcohol in his bloodstream above the legal limit / think of the ravages of lung cancer / nine-tenths of lung cancer victims are smokers / and smoking of course brings about not only lung cancer / but heart disease and bronchitis too / first problem drug abuse / our second problem is obesity / obesity brought about by **an overindulgence in certain foods / especially saturated fats** / and a lack of exercise / our Victorian ancestors had few of the labour saving devices that we enjoy today *thatwethatweprofitfromtoday* / of which the car is the perhaps the chief offender / lack of exercise / overindulgence in saturated fats / bring about obesity / and obesity leads to heart disease / back problems and so on / dental decay /

dental decay is the most prevalent disease in the United Kingdom today / 36 million fillings are made every year by British dentists / partially due to bad eating habits / but also due to poor dental hygiene / all of these problems raise the question of how far should individuals be free to harm themselves / when society has to deal with and pay for the consequences / another major target for preventive medicine today is the problems of old age / ironically the problems of old age in our society are due in part to the very success of curative and preventive medicine / if we think **back to Victorian times** / the median age of death in the early Victorian period was 48 / and today it's around 75 for men / so one of the main targets for preventive medicine today must be to keep old people mobile / keep them out of hospital / finally I've put down / as targets for preventive medicine / mental illness / 5 million visits are made to doctors' surgeries each year in this country by patients complaining of mental illness / these then are the targets for preventive medicine today in the United Kingdom / drug abuse / obesity / dental decay / the problems of old age / and mental health /

now let's consider the problems of the developing countries / and we'll start with some of the problems that we share with the developing nations / both the developing and the developed nations suffer from bad diet / I've already talked about overindulgence in saturated fats and carbohydrates in the West / a problem of **TOO MUCH** / in the developing countries the problem is one of **TOO LITTLE** / problems which lead to undernutrition or malnutrition / often / like ourselves / the problem is due not to a **LACK** of food / but due to an **UNBALANCED** diet / the lack of certain components in the diet /

other problems that are shared between the developing and developed nations are the problems of tobacco addiction and alcoholism / I suppose the third most obvious problem for preventive medicine to tackle in the developing world / is the problem of uncontrolled population growth / there's the danger that food supplies **may be outstripped by** population increases /

and fourthly / there are problems of disease / malaria, leprosy, tuberculosis and of course HIV / where can we begin to tackle this problem / in the developing countries? / resources are limited / it is important that the most efficient strategy for success be employed as early as possible /

let's consider / let's take as a case history the problem of malaria / how do we eliminate malaria? / now there are three possible preventive measures / the first one would be to drain the marshes / *getridof thewetplaces wherethemosquitobreedsandthrives* / the second strategy would be to kill the mosquitoes themselves / *spraythemwithinsecticide* / and the third strategy would be to give all the people living in the affected areas anti-malarial drugs to take / and notice / that we've three possible strategies / and not one of them involves the medical practitioner directly / it's the task of the civil engineer to drain the marshes / the important role in killing mosquitoes is played by <u>the man with the spray gun</u> / who goes round the houses spraying the walls and the ceilings / and the key figure in distributing anti-malarial drugs is <u>the health visitor</u> / finally there's the problem of the individual himself / who must / who must take the drugs / *willheinfacttakethedrugs?* especially if these are anti-malarial drugs / especially if these are pressed on him by <u>well-meaning but</u> foreign personnel /

we can see the same / problem of choice of strategies / in the problem of <u>improved nutrition</u> / how do you get a better diet for people? / one strategy would be to introduce new crops / the task of <u>the agronomist</u> / another might be to irrigate / um and that's the task of the engineer / in some countries the major problem is that uncontrolled rain brings flooding / and that <u>creates landslides</u> and so on / the answer there might be <u>afforestation</u> or contour-terracing / and again / that's not the <u>province</u> of the medical practitioner / and **at the end of the day** again we have the problem of the individual / you can persuade the farmer to grow new crops / you can irrigate the fields to help farmers to do so / but **at the end of the day** you must persuade the farmer and his family to eat them / and one of the major problems is persuading people to change their food habits / people are at their most <u>conservative</u> when they're concerned with filling their stomachs /

we can see then / some of the similarities and some of the differences between preventive medicine in the developing countries and in the developed countries / now **for my money** the most effective strategy in both the developed and the developing countries is health education / health education must come first / you must educate people to smoke less / to drink in moderation / you must educate people to change their food habits / to take a different diet / you must educate people to take prophylactic drugs / such as anti-malarial tablets / so / in conclusion we can see that / there are differences between the developing and the developed worlds in the task of preventive medicine / but for both / the solution seems to be health education / thank you very much /

Handout: **Targets for Preventive Medicine**

Outline
1 Improvements in health in UK
2 Problems remaining
3 Targets for developing countries

1. Improvements in health in UK

Changes

100 yrs ago... *four out of every ten children died in childhood*
survivors faced diseases
poorer people suffered nutritional deficiencies (e.g. rickets)
all classes vulnerable to water-borne diseases (e.g. typhoid, cholera)

today... *UK pop has doubled (despite 50% fall in birth rate)*
very few families lose a child

healthier today because of preventive med., not curative

Factors
- immunization
    against diphtheria, tetanus, whooping cough, polio

- infant clinics
    health visitors, better nursing and midwifery standards

- screening measures
    e.g. for TB

- the 'Sanitary Revolution'
    (Public Health Act 1875) piped water
    cheap soap
    public bath-houses + wash-houses
    cotton underclothes

- *better diet*

- *birth control*

- *working cond'ns (Factory Acts)*

2. Problems remaining
   - Drug abuse   *alcohol + tobacco*

   - Obesity   *esp. saturated fats + lack of exercise*
     obesity leads to heart disease, back problems

   - Dental decay   *36m fillings*

   - Old age   *ironically, due to success of medicine:*
     in 19thC ave. age of death was 48 yrs for men, now around 75

   - Mental illness   *5m visits to doctors*

3. Targets for developing countries

   - Diet   *problem of too little (in West, too much)*
     unbalanced diet

   - Tobacco & alc.   *both dev'ing and dev'd nations*

   - Pop. growth   *risk that food supplies may be inadequate for pop. increase*

   - Disease   *malaria, leprosy, TB, HIV*

Choice of strategies – example: Malaria

Three poss. strats: *1. drain marshes where mosquitoes live*
                       2. kill mosquitoes with insecticide
                       3. give anti-malarial drugs

NB none of these strats involves the doctor

       problem of individual – will he take the drugs?

Choice of strategies – example: Improved nutrition

Poss. strats: *1. introduce new crops (task of agronomist)*
                     2. irrigate (engineer)
                     3. afforestation
                     Again, none of these involves the doctor
                     Again, the problem of the individual: will farmers change their diet?

Most effective strategy:
       in both dev'd and dev'ing countries – HEALTH EDUCATION

Unit 6 Cloning: the significance of Dolly

HARRY GRIFFIN

Dolly the sheep was the first mammal cloned from an adult cell / she was born on the fifth of July 1996 / and the announcement of her birth / uh about seven months later / started uh what has been an enduring fascination by the media and the public at large with all things cloned / uh in this talk / I want to describe the technique by which Dolly was created and reflect uh on how the technology has developed / **or perhaps hasn't developed** / uh over the intervening five or six years / uh and then review very briefly the practical applications / uh of cloning / and try and separate / uh those that are likely / from those that have uh / attracted a lot of speculation uh and uh media interest /

Dolly was created by a technique called *nuclear transfer* / and most of the manipulations involved are done by looking down a microscope and using micro-manipulators / <u>a first step</u> <u>is to</u> take an unfertilised egg / and using pipettes to suck out / uh the maternal nucleus / **once that's been done** / the DNA is replaced / by inserting a cell / in Dolly's case uh from the mammary gland / back in place of the maternal nucleus that's been removed / the end-product of this sequence is in essence / uh a cell a body cell a mammary gland cell uh within an egg / and this reconstructed embryo is activated and the two cells fused together / by a small electric pulse / and in a small proportion of cases / this reconstructed embryo begins to divide and multiply / just as a normal embryo would do / in the experiment uh in which Dolly was created / over 400 eggs were used / 277 reconstructed embryos were created and of these only about ten per cent developed into blastocysts / that is the stage of embryonic development where there may be 100 to 120 cells / of the 29 uh

cloned embryos that developed into blastocysts / they were implanted into 13 surrogate mothers / only one of which became pregnant /

at first Dolly was a clone alone and there was a tremendous amount of **speculation** about whether or not the experiment could ever be repeated / or indeed whether we'd made a **mistake** / uh in creating Dolly not from an adult cell but from a foetal cell / and there were one or two suggestions that Dolly was simply **a fake** / all this **speculation** came to the uh an end in the summer of 1998 when a group in Hawaii reported uh the cloning of over 50 mice / and since then uh research groups around the world have cloned cattle, sheep, goats, more mice, rabbits / and pigs / and there's one example of a cloned kitten / equally competent groups have tried to clone other species and been unsuc… **unsuccessful** so far / as far as cloning rats, dogs or monkeys / and overall the success rate of cloning is <u>**very**</u> <u>**low**</u> / less than one per cent on average of cloned embryos make it to term / many cloned embryos uh **fail to develop** at all / when they do develop to blastocysts some cloned embryos **fail to implant** / and even when the surrogate mother becomes pregnant carrying a cloned embryo / **failures can occur** throughout gestation / up to and including birth /

there are a number of well uh / characterised **problems** with cloning / in cattle and sheep / there's a tendency for the offspring to be **oversized** / perhaps up to twice or more the size of normal embryos uh when they are born / in mice / uh the cloned mice seem to be a normal size / but the placenta can be **twice or three times uh normal size** / problems persist uh after birth / cloned mice for example **tend**

to obesity / and there is one reported study uh of cloned mice **dying about two-thirds of the way through a normal lifespan** / other problems reported in clones uh include **failure** of the lungs to develop / or **failure** of the immune system uh a few weeks after birth / and there has been uh **questions raised about whether any clone is entirely normal** / and it's clearly going to be uh a long time before we can be sure that cloned animals <u>can</u> be normal / studies need to be carried / through uh a complete lifespan / which is clearly much easier than / in mice than in a long-lived species like uh cattle /

the reasons for the problems associated with cloning uh **boil down to** whether or not the adult cell introduced **into the enucleated oocyte** is appropriately reprogrammed / normally uh embryos are produced by fusion of eggs and sperm / uh the DNA of which has been matured uh over years and months uh before the fertilisation occurs / the situation is very different with cloning / because the DNA introduced into the oocyte uh is from a specialised cell / a mammary gland cell for example may have thirty or forty thousand genes / but **most of them have been silenced** / uh because they are / not used uh in the functioning of the mammary gland / what's being expected of that cell of that DNA / is that once it's transferred to / an enucleated oocyte those silent genes are reawakened / and within a very short time / a matter of hours / they're expected to behave as they would do normally / uh in a / embryo created by fertilisation / it's not therefore surprising that if some genes are inappropriately regulated / uh come on during development uh too late or too strong / then uh normal development **is compromised** / most research groups working in this area now are concerned with trying to understand the basic mechanisms uh behind the reprogramming process / on the basis that if we can understand that / we can improve the success rates of cloning from the current one / perhaps one to two per cent in some species / uh to make it a more viable uh more reliable process /

most of the **PUBLIC** fascination most of the **MEDIA** fascination / uh with cloning has been / along the lines 'is it **POSSIBLE** to clone a human **BEING**?' / and certainly uh experience with a range of species suggests that in **THEORY** at least it should be possible to clone a **CHILD** / whether or not this is a **SENSIBLE** thing to do in the **LONG** term / uh is uh a matter of considerable ethical **DEBATE** / certainly at the **MOMENT ALL** the evidence / from experiments with animals suggests that this would be a **RISKY** procedure / not just for the prospective **CHILD** but also for uh the **MOTHER** carrying that child / and it would be wholly **IRRESPONSIBLE** using the technology uh at its **PRESENT** state of development / for anybody to attempt to uh clone a **CHILD** /

our own motivation at the Roslin Institute uh for cloning / or developing the technology at least / was to produce / uh uh develop a better way of genetically modifying farm animal species / cloning in essence converts cells / cells that can be cultured / but cells into live animals / and if those cells are first genetically modified / then the clones produced from those cells will be genetically modified too / and this approach has already been used to insert genes at a specific point in the genome / uh milk protein genes / uh in order to produce human proteins in the milk of transgenic sheep and cattle / and it's also been used to delete genes / so in the case of pigs / for example / uh / cloning has been used to delete a gene which is responsible for the uh rejection of a pig organ by uh a human patient / the context here is xenotransplantation / the possibility of using genetically modified pigs uh to address the shortfall of / organs for transplant to human patients / and it's very clear that if xenotransplantation is going to be successful then it is the precision uh that uh the genetic modifications using cloning uh can provide / that will make uh the technology ultimately successful // cloning is normally / uh associated with the idea of replicating or copying animals / and indeed there are research groups and companies in Australia and New Zealand Japan / and the United States uh trying to develop the technology to clone cattle and to specifically uh copy the very best-performing animals / at the moment the cost of producing such animals is very high and it's going to need uh / a lot of ingenuity / a lot of practical development to reduce the costs / to make this a commercial proposition uh in normal cattle production // cloning has also been suggested as a way of preserving endangered species / uh and while this may have very positive vibes in public relations terms uh this is highly likely <u>not</u> to be a practical way forward / one of the requirements uh to clone an animal is a supply of eggs and a uh an availability of surrogate mothers to carry the cloned embryos to term / it's been suggested for example uh that uh rabbits might provide a source of eggs for cloning pandas / which would then be implanted uh in cats uh acting as surrogate mothers / uh the chance of such uh cross-species uh cloning experiments working uh must be close to zero / and there must be much better ways / uh more pragmatic ways of trying to preserve the panda uh than resorting to very high-tech solutions / uh with little chance of success // even more imaginatively is the idea that you might use cloning to resurrect extinct species / here we're very much uh / in the realms of 'Jurassic Park' / which I would remind uh the audience is a work of fiction / uh not uh a scientific treatise / the

idea that you might resurrect the Tasmanian tiger / uh a marsupial that's been uh extinct for over 40 years / uh by taking a DNA sample from a / uh (*coughs*) uh DNA from a sample that's been in a bottle of alcohol uh for 150 years has been mooted by one Australian museum / this sort of project has no chance of success / uh the DNA in such material is hopelessly fragmented and the idea that you might reconstruct a complete genome from it is simply fanciful /

given that the practical uh benefits / certainly as seen now / uh for uh cloning seem to be rather uh **limited** / why has cloning excited the scientific community as well as the media? / well the birth of Dolly / uh was a seminal event / it demonstrated uh in uh spectacular fashion uh that the cells in our bodies / are far more versatile than we previously thought / we all start life as a single cell / as a fertilised egg / uh that cell divides and multiplies as the embryo uh develops / as the embryo uh / progresses towards a a foetus and the foetus to an animal / and that single cell becomes uh many billions of cells / of perhaps two or three hundred different cell types / and that process of gradual differentiation was presumed by developmental biologists / at least as far as mammals are concerned / to be irreversible / it was a one-way process / Dolly was created from a mammary gland cell / and / uh provided uh spectacular evidence that the cells in our bodies are capable of being de-differentiated / uh of having their clock turned back / uh back to zero / and to start life all over again / the practical benefits of this knowledge are uncertain / it certainly provides us with a tremendous new insight uh into uh our bodies / perhaps uh a great insight into how repair mechanisms are mobilised uh in case of human illness / and potentially has applications in new therapies based on stem cells / uh for treatment of diseases like

Parkinson's uh heart attack and stroke / so in thirty years time / **we will have either accepted** that cloning uh is an appropriate though **limited** tool to help infertile couples / or perhaps **forgotten** about the application at all / but hopefully we will still have / this understanding about the versatility of the cells in our bodies / and it will be that / that uh Dolly will be remembered for / rather uh than all the media **speculation** about whether anyone is going to clone a child / and who's doing it or when / thank you /

Dolly: sample notes

Intro

Dolly first mammal cloned from adult cell (5 July 1996)
started fascination by media and public

Outline: 1. describe clon. techn.
2. say how techn. has dev'd (or not) since Dolly
3. review pract. applic'ns

Nuclear transfer

1. take maternal nucleus from unfertilised egg
2. insert an adult cell into egg
3. active new (reconstructed) embryo and fuse with cell
4. (in few cases) embryo begins to divide and multiply

Speculation: Dolly

Could the exp't be repeated?
Was it a mistake? (Had they used a foetal cell, not adult one?)
Was it a fake?

Other clones

mice (Hawaii '98), cattle, sheep, goats, rabbits. pigs, cat (kitten)
BUT very low success rate

Problems with cloning

offspring oversized; or placenta oversized
mice tend to obesity
tend to die early
failure of lungs, or of immune system

Sources of problems

Success depends on whether the adult cell can be properly 'reprogrammed'.
Adult cells = specialised, by having certain genes 'silenced'
Cloning with adult cells requires cells to 'have their clock turned back,
to reawaken' the silent genes

Human cloning?

in theory, possible
but ethical debate
at pres., evid. from animal exp'ts = wd be risky for child and mother
so <u>wholly irresponsible</u> at moment to try to clone a child

Motivation for cloning

1. At Roslin Institute – to find better way of genet. modifying farm animals (modify cells before cloning, e.g. to produce animals making human proteins)
2. (Roslin) Xenotransplantation: GM pigs to provide hearts for human transplants
3. (Elsewhere) Copying best-performing animals – but very expensive
4. Preserving endangered species – but not practical
5. Resurrect (revive) extinct species – no chance of success

Importance of Dolly

Dolly exp't showed that body cells are versatile – that their programming (specialis'n) can be reversed (clocks turned back)

Conclusion: balancing the picture

If practical benefits uncertain, what have we gained?

Insight into our bodies – esp. repair mechanisms
May be useful for treating disease

In 30 yrs, <u>EITHER</u> cloning will be a limited tool for treating infertility
    <u>OR</u> perhaps it will have been forgotten

Dolly will be remembered for increasing our understanding,
    not for starting speculation about human cloning

Unit 7 Measuring quality of life

MAURICEA LIMA LYNCH

good morning / what I'd like to do in this uh short talk is to discuss some of the ways uh researchers try to measure quality of life or well-being and the difficulties with such measures /

one simple definition of quality of life links it to the fulfilment of personal goals / of course the perception of high or low quality of life is subjective and may differ from individual to individual / **researchers from different fields** have attempted to measure quality of life / concentrating on different dimensions of life according to their particular areas of interest / **psychologists** have tried to measure quality of life by studying subjective well-being and attempting to develop national indices of happiness / in the area of uh **health service research**, hundreds of different research instruments / mainly based on questionnaires / have been developed to measure quality of life of patients after medical treatment / **the vast number of instruments** used to measure health-related quality of life / indicates **the methodological problems** that researchers have encountered in trying to find a valid and reliable measure which can be used in a way that is really meaningful /

quality of life of course does not **relate** only to health status but is in fact multi-dimensional / it relates to physical, **mental**, economic and social well-being / when we move from the **domain** of the individual to international comparisons of quality of life / we find that the methodological **difficulties** become even greater /

traditionally / economists have used levels of standard of living as **indicators** of quality of life among countries and or within countries / for most of the 20th century the only

measurement used to compare the standards of living of **citizens** of different countries was national income / this was often **criticised** for various reasons / the main one being that standard of living should not be analysed only in terms of economic growth / in the second half of the 20th century economists and other social scientists started to develop indices which **included** social as well as economic indicators / the aim of these indices was to give a more holistic picture of the living conditions of different **populations** / in this context the terms 'quality of life', 'social well-being' and 'human development' seem to be used **interchangeably** /

the best-known of these indices is the United Nations' Human Development Index / or HDI / which was first published in 1990 / and I'd like to take a few minutes to talk about this particular index / the HDI is described in the UN Human Development Report for 2002 as a 'simple summary measure of three dimensions of the human development concept: living a long and healthy life, being educated and having a decent standard of living' / so there are three parts to this particular index / long and healthy life, education and standard of living / now / the concept of living a long and healthy life is captured by life expectancy at birth / although / life expectancy does measure length of life it doesn't necessarily reflect health status / in other words it isn't always true that individuals who live longer are also healthy / in particular in the last years of life /

educational attainment is measured in the HDI by two indicators / by adult literacy rates that is the proportion of people aged at least 15 years old who can read and write a short simple statement on their everyday life / and also by the ratio of combined enrolments in primary, secondary and tertiary education /

the final element in the HDI is standard of living and that is measured in terms of Gross Domestic Product per capita / that is GDP / divided by the total population /

so how is the index calculated? / well it is calculated by averaging the values of those three dimensions of human development / life expectancy, educational attainment and standard of living / tables are then produced containing as many countries as possible / normally, the number of countries uh which appear in these tables is restricted by the availability of data / although some countries with incomplete data do still appear in the tables /

the United Nations Report for 2002 gives indices for 173 countries / as you can see from the handout the Report puts Norway and Sweden at the top of the list / of what are called the 'most livable countries' / um Canada comes third, Australia fifth and the United Kingdom 13th / of the 25 most livable countries 17 are in Europe / at the other end of the table the 25 least livable countries are all in Africa / now um **no doubt you have your own views as to** whether or not these rankings are meaningful /

it is widely recognised that measuring only those three dimensions leaves out other very important aspects of human development / and one of the criticisms of the UN index is that / the number of factors included is **too limited** / there are some other difficulties with the index / um / I don't have time to discuss them all but I will briefly mention some of them / um firstly there is the problem of what the index **is actually measuring** / for example poverty is obviously a major contributor to poor quality of life / but the devastating

consequences of absolute poverty are not transparent in measures like GDP per capita / neither is **the extent of income inequalities** / another important exclusion is the **net effect of economic growth on the environment** and its **impact on quality of life** / secondly there is the issue of the **quality and quantity of the information** collected / the same methodology for data collection is not strictly applied in all countries / and the gaps in the tables used for the calculation of the index / show that some components of the index are actually **based on guesstimates** / a third question we should ask is how well the Western concepts used in social well-being indices um reflect the way that individuals in non-Western cultures perceive their quality of life / this can be illustrated by a discussion in Schumacher's book 'Small is Beautiful', when he compared modern economics / by which he meant Western economics / and Buddhist economics / he argued that Western economics measures standard of living by the amount of annual consumption / assuming all the time that a person who consumes more / is better off than another who consumes less / on the other hand a Buddhist economist would see this as irrational / since consumption is merely a means to human well-being / the aim should be to obtain the maximum of well-being with the minimum of consumption / so um higher GDP per capita would not be a meaningful indicator of greater human development in Buddhist economics / finally um we have to ask whether the researchers / and government officials who um develop aggregate measures of uh quality of life are really in touch with the perceptions of ordinary citizens as to what quality of life or human development is about /

there is an interesting example of this uh from Scotland / in 2001 a piece of research was commissioned by the government with the objective of uh understanding the aspirations of people living in Scotland / they were asked questions like / 'What are the most important changes you'd hope to see in Scotland in the next 10 years in order to improve the quality of people's lives?' / 'What are the two or three most important things that should be done in order to achieve this vision of the future?' / the themes identified by the research included **issues to do with** physical and mental health / full employment and financial security / a pollution-free environment / good housing, a drug-free Scotland and safety and security / the results of the research were then summarised and presented to a small group of leading decision-makers / and influential people in Scotland uh for discussion / everybody in the group except one / considered the level of ambition expressed by the public **to be disappointed** / although um not surprising / some of them commented um that the people

had very limited ambitions / and a natural resistance to change / so / even in a country like Scotland which has a relatively small and affluent population / those who make decisions affecting people's / quality of life / can be **out of touch with** what ordinary citizens perceive as improvements in the quality of their lives / you may have examples of similar mismatches in your own country /

so / in conclusion / when we look at league tables of uh countries ranked according to quality of life / measured by a single figure **we need to be very cautious** about how meaningful they are / we should uh ask ourselves whether these aggregate indices / can really represent quality of life or social well-being / of individuals with such different socio-economic, political, cultural and religious traditions and experiences /

Measuring Quality of Life

Dimensions of Quality of Life

- Physical

- Mental

- Economic

- Social

UN Human Development Index Definition

"Simple summary measure of three dimensions of the human development concept: living a long and healthy life, being educated and having a decent standard of living"

(Human Development Report, 2002; p. 34)

Q of L – subjective

researchers conc. on diff. dimensions

method. problems

- indiv. v intern'l comparisons
  ↓ greater method. diffs.
- Econ'ists used stand. of living as indicator: national income
  → various criticisms

Later in 20c – econ'ists + other soc. scientists used more holistic measures

Q of L = soc. well-being = human dev't

Dimensions Measured in the UN Human Development Index

- **long and healthy life** → life expectancy at birth

- **education** → adult literacy rates combined primary, secondary and tertiary education enrolment ratios

- **standard of living** → GDP per capita

Life exp. measures length of life but not health

Lit. rates = prop'n of people over 15 able to read and write

HDI = ave. of three dimensions

UN Human Development Report 2002 "Most Livable Countries"

1.	Norway	14.	Denmark
2.	Sweden	15.	Austria
3.	Canada	16.	Luxembourg
4.	Belgium	17.	Germany
5.	Australia	18.	Ireland
6.	United States	19.	New Zealand
7.	Iceland	20.	Italy
8.	Netherlands	21.	Spain
9.	Japan	22.	Israel
10.	Finland	23.	Hong Kong, China
11.	Switzerland	24.	Greece
12.	France	25.	Singapore
13.	United Kingdom		

Source: United Nations Human Development Report, 2002. New York: United Nations.

UN HDI for 173 countries

NB 17 of these in Europe

UN Human Development Report 2002 "Least Livable Countries"

1.	Sierra Leone	14.	Gambia
2.	Niger	15.	Guinea
3.	Burundi	16.	Benin
4.	Mozambique	17.	Eritrea
5.	Burkin Faso	18.	Côte d'Ivoire
6.	Ethiopia	19.	Congo, Dem. Rep. of
7.	Guinea-Bissau	20.	Senegal
8.	Chad	21.	Zambia
9.	Central African Republic	22.	Mauritania
10.	Mali	23.	Tanzania
11.	Malawi	24.	Uganda
12.	Rwanda	25.	Djibouti
13.	Angola		

Source: United Nations Human Development Report, 2002. New York: United Nations.

All in Africa

(is this meaningful?)

Concerns over the HDI Index

- Exclusion of important factors in determining quality of life/human development
- Differences in the quality and availability of the international data
- Meaningfulness of the index as an indicator of global human development

GDP per capita: doesn't show eff's of absolute pov. or env. effects

Not same methodol. used by all countries; data unavail. — GUESSTIMATES

Diffs. in perceptions of Q of L

- Western v. non-West cultures
  West: ↑ consumption = ↑ Q of L
  Buddhist: max. well being with
  econ.   min. consumption

Useful References

- Brink S and Zeesman A (1997) Measuring Social Well-Being: An Index of Social Health for Canada. http://www.hrdc-drhc.gc.ca/sp-ps/arb-dgra/publications/research/r-97-9e.pdf

- United Nations. Human Development Report, 2002. New York: United Nations. http://www.undp.org/hdr2002

▷ Mismatch betw. perceptions of researchers/officials and ordinary citizens,
EVEN WITHIN SAME CULTURE

Unit 8 Climate change: evidence and action

SIMON ALLEN

I'm going to talk to you today about climate change / because I think it's one of the most serious problems that faces humanity at the beginning of the 21st century / climate change seems to be **on everybody's lips these days** / quite frequently in the news media we hear about extreme re… weather events / floods / droughts / strange snowfalls / and **increasingly people are questioning** whether these are actual na… actually natural events or they're perhaps the result of the impacts of Man's activities on the Earth's climate / but what I want to know is / if there's apparently **such widespread concern and belief** about climate change / why is it apparently so difficult for international governments to tackle? / so in this talk I'm going to start off by / reviewing the evidence for believing that climate change is a real phenomenon and is actually happening / and then I'm going to go on to think about why is it so difficult to get international action to address climate change /

so / turning to the evidence / my comments are going to draw on the most recent report from the Intergovernmental Panel on Climate Change / this is an international panel of scientific experts that was set up in 1988 by the United Nations and the World Meteorological Office / to advise governments on / the current state of knowledge / concerning the climate system / the report they made in 2001 is the most recent and most authoritative overview of the state of climate science / there are really three main types of evidence that confirm our belief in climate change / firstly there are observations / people have measured the climate since about 1850 / the climate is of course interesting particularly to farmers / so / as soon as the thermometer was invented people started to measure temperature on a

regular basis / these measurements of temperature show that through the 20th century / global temperature global mean average surface temperature has increased by about 0.6 degrees centigrade / earlier in previous reports from the IPCC there was some doubt about / whether um temperature change of this magnitude had actually occurred / because people said that they were biased / there was bias in the temperature records / primarily coming from the *urban heat island effect* / that is, that many of the temperature measuring stations are close to cities / and cities have uh have climates that are not the same as the average climate over the earth's surface / because a great deal of energy use takes place in cities / and so / city climates are a little bit warmer than / um / than the general rural climate / so some people claimed that / the apparent increase in temperature could be just due to the effect of urban… urbanisation on the temperature recording system _//_ but in the most recent report / the global temperature dataset has been very carefully quality controlled and corrected to this effect / and there's now / um increasing confidence that / a temperature change of that order has indeed occurred _//_ but as well as these measurements it is also possible to reconstruct temperature back in time / from other so-called *proxy measures* / there are / many natural organisms that uh / they leave traces of their previous activities in the environment / that we can look at today / we can measure the uh thickness of tree rings and the growth of trees is responsive to temperature and / rainfall / we can also look at the width of bandings in corals / and we can even extract information from lake sediments **and ice cores** / so putting all the data of this type together it's been possible to reconstruct / the changes in temperature over the whole of the last millennium / this data shows very clearly that the 20th century was very much warmer than the previous 900 years / **from the ice core** data alone it's possible to reconstruct temperature back to 420,000 years ago / and these data show that / the temperature now is / warmer than any time during that period /

a second line of evidence is to actually look / at / the trends / in the greenhouse gases in the atmosphere / **greenhouse gases are responsible for trapping heat within the Earth's atmosphere** / this is a natural phenomenon / the most important greenhouse gases are water vapour and carbon dioxide / and these have always been present in the atmosphere / they have the effect of reducing the rate at which heat is lost from Earth's surface out into space / so they keep the Earth much warmer than it would be if it didn't have an atmosphere / **if it wasn't for this natural greenhouse effect / the global surface temperature would be something like minus 15 degrees centigrade** / so life as we know it could not exist / the problem is that man's activities are increasing the concentration of greenhouse gases / the most significant man-made increase is coming through carbon dioxide / carbon dioxide is emitted from any kind of activity that's based on the combustion of fossil fuels / so any any kind of um power generation / heating / uh use of vehicles / anything that burns oil, coal or gas / causes an increase in carbon dioxide / and since the industrial revolution the um concentration has increased very rapidly / um about 31 per cent since 1750 / so again turning to the data from the ice cores / we can see two things / firstly that the current carbon dioxide concentration is / clearly much higher than the concentration has been over the whole of the previous 420,000 years / also interestingly over that

period the Earth's mean surface temperature has varied / and so has the carbon dioxide concentration / and there seems to be a very tight relationship between the two / as one increases so does the other / and this gives us confidence that um / it's likely that if we change / through human activities the carbon dioxide concentration / that temperature will change / accordingly /

so the / final third / line of evidence that gives us concern about climate change / is the evidence that comes from the use of climate models / these are very complicated computer models which aim to simulate the whole of the climate system / that is, the interactions between / the atmospheric circulation, the oceans, the land surface and the the ice that is present in polar regions / the Earth system is very complex and not all of the processes can be represented adequately / either because they're not very well-known or just that it would make the models too complicated to run on current computers / but as time's passed / the models **have been refined** become and become **more detailed** / and / we now have **more confidence** in their ability to predict the future **accurately** / partly this has come from the fact that the models can now predict the recent changes in climate **fairly accurately** / the models have been changed so that they take into account some of the natural influences on climate / that some people used to claim could be responsible for the apparent climate change / things like the 11-year sun spot cycle which changes the output from the sun / or the effect of aerosol in the atmosphere that comes from volcanic eruptions like Mount Pinatubo / very small particles suspended in the atmosphere / reflect radiation out into space and can have a cooling effect / **but these things have been factored in now** / and we can get a good match between climate model simulations and the past / and that **gives us**

confidence in their use to predict the future / we can also use them as tools to quantify the natural variability in the climate system / one of the problems / of proving that climate change through human agency has actually occurred / is that / the climate is naturally inherently very variable / and the changes we're looking for are quite small / the mean changes are quite small compared with that natural pattern of variability / but now with climate models we've been able to quantify and understand the variability / and we can see that / the changes in temperature that have occurred / particularly over the last 50 years are very unlikely to have been to have arisen through natural factors /

so if we accept that climate change is going to occur / what does it mean for human society? / well some of the consequences could be quite unpleasant / uh climate change will cause sea-level rise / and many low-lying coastal areas / some of which are very densely populated / will be vulnerable to inundation / through storms and storm surges / there could be serious effects on agriculture / particularly in / tropical countries where the climate is already warm and arid / and any increase in temperature and aridity will have serious impacts on crop yields / there'll be impacts on natural ecosystems / we could perhaps see serious die-back of tropical rain-forests or the loss of coral reefs / due to due to warming of the water / these are two of the most / diverse types of ecosystems on the planet /

so there's a lot to be concerned about / and as I mentioned before / one hears people talk about climate change as if it's a real phenomena and it's going to occur / but not very much seems to be happening internationally to address the problem / in 1997 / the world's governments met and negotiated the / Kyoto Protocol on climate change / and this set up um a series of targets for emission reductions that governments / at least the governments of industrialised countries / would be obl… would be obliged to meet by 2012 / **in any case / the targets were rather weak** / amounting to something like a five per cent reduction in emissions / when most climate scientists believe that something like a 60 per cent reduction in emissions would be required to stabilise / the concentration of CO_2 in the atmosphere / so as it stood / the agreement wasn't likely to correct the problem / **it was just a small step in the right direction** / but recently **the United States of America pulled out of the agreement** / and this's had a major impact / it's likely that it will be impossible to get the agreement ratified by enough countries / for it actually to come into force and for the targets to become / legally enforceable / and **the loss of the United States from the negotiations has allowed other / sceptical countries / to water down the provisions** and / increase the size of the numerous loopholes that already existed in the agreement / so the future doesn't look too good /

so / let's just look at some of the reasons why it's very difficult to get an in… international action on climate change / the first problem is that the science is complex / there're lots of different / well there're several different kinds of greenhouse gases they come from a range of different activities / they're going to have a lot of different impacts / the picture is very difficult / particularly for the general public to understand / the debate in the public media has been clouded by disinformation campaigns sponsored by people comp… / primarily large companies who have an interest in the status quo / companies uh like the oil giants / power generating utilities / car companies / they've paid um lobbyists to try to undermine the outputs of um the climate scientists and have caused confusion in the public mind about whether or not climate change is really a serious problem / the media hasn't helped the situation / the media likes to present any kind of issue as a debate between conflicting interest groups / so **although** the media's provided a channel for the consensus view of climate scientists to be presented / it's always chosen representatives from lobby groups to put up against them / and the general public rarely realise that the climate scientists represent a consensus of / hundreds of scientific experts / who are pretty independent-minded / **whereas** the lobbyists represent a small group of powerful companies and have a very particular agenda /

the second problem in getting international action is that climate change / is primarily caused by / the burning of fossil fuels also to some extent by land use changes caused by agriculture / the use of energy and agriculture are **absolutely key underpinnings of modern society** / the development of modern economies is very closely linked with energy use / there's **a very close coupling** between energy use and standard measurements of economic progress like gross domestic product / so the idea that we might have to / in industrialised societies move away from fossil fuels / and produce all the goods and services that we currently enjoy / from renewable energy / is a very very daunting / very difficult prospect / it suggests a radical restructuring of society that many people find **just too daunting** / and when you consider the very short horizon on which most governments plan for the future / in de… democratic countries elections / perhaps only occur every five years or something like that / it's very hard for governments to **contemplate changes in society** / which / may produce / reductions in the quality of life / as perceived by many of their citizens / so doing something about

climate change **threatens the status quo** / it threatens the most powerful countries /

and the third problem is that / climate change is really / a problem that results from the activities of the rich industrialised countries / but the effects are primarily going to be felt by the people / mainly poor people / who live in developing countries / particularly the people who live on small island states / like the atolls in the South Pacific / where / the land surface is nowhere more than a few metres above sea level / and even fairly small changes in sea level / will thr… completely threaten the future existence of their countries / or the people in Bangladesh and Egypt who live / um in the highly populated coastal areas / threatened by coastal flooding / or the semi-arid tropical countries where food security is already a problem / and reductions in rainfall and increases in temperature will bring further water scarcity and problems for agriculture / these are the people who're going to suffer / the countries responsible for the pollution / mainly are in the northern hemisphere / where / the impacts will be less / and more importantly / the countries have strong economies and will be able to take actions necessary to adapt to the impacts of climate change / for instance / reinforcing flood defences / or strengthening infrastructure to cope with increased storm possible increased storm damage / all all kinds of measures are more feasible **when there's money around to fund them** / so / to do something about climate change it requires / people / who are not going to suffer / or believe that they won't suffer very much / to care about people in far away places that they hardly even know / **and not even the people who are around now** / but the developed world needs to care for future generations / the as yet unborn who live in these countries / this is very hard to achieve /

so / **how can how can we** make progress / in dealing with climate change? / well **we might be** frustrated by what's happening on the international scene / things seem to be going too slowly / the measures contemplated aren't strong enough / but at least we as individuals **can do something** to reduce our own greenhouse gas emissions / the United Kingdom for instance / has or a target under Kyoto / to reduce its emissions by / 12.5 per cent by 2012 / and it's imposed a stronger domestic target to reduce CO_2 emissions by 20 per cent / just about every individual living in the UK **could easily achieve** those reductions themselves / just by / reducing / their own use of fossil fuel energy / by installing energy efficiency measures in their house / even relatively cheap energy-efficient light bulbs / by using their cars less or not at all / um just walking or cycling or using public transport / by making sure that they buy their electricity from people who're offering renewable energy / these measures are all possible now / and if everyone took them **they could have a** significant impact / but in the long term we need action internationally / and I'm not sure how this is going to happen / but I think the governments of developed countries need to realise that we're all in the same boat together /

and / although / the direct impacts / **may be ones that** / developed countries could cope with / we live in a very interlinked global economy now / and / impacts in far away places **could still affect us** / through reductions in availability of agricultural products / through international flows of environmental refugees / and the events of September 11 / the terrorist attacks in the USA / remind us that disaffected people in far distant parts of the world **can represent a major threat** to our stability and security / so **it might be wise** to avoid / or do something to reduce / what **could be** disastrous impacts of climate change on some developing countries /

so it's my hope that / the developed countries will realise / that it's important to help developing countries / develop their economies and base them on / non-fossil fuel intensive means of production / so that their quality of life **can be improved** but without increasing greenhouse gas emissions to dangerous levels / but the biggest challenge is that simultaneously / developed countries are going to have to / reduce their own emissions and this **may ultimately mean** reductions in the level of personal consumption /

Climate change (CC): sample notes

Intro   CC = serious problem
1. review evidence
2. why so diff. to get int'l action?

IPCC report 2001 – authorit. overview

Types of evidence for CC
1. observations **of temp. and** proxy measures **(tree rings, coral, ice cores)**
2. 'a second line of evidence' **trends in greenhouse gases (GGs)**
       ice cores: CO_2 **highest for 420,000 yrs**

                 temp has varied with CO_2
3. **computer models: complex, but now refined – so more confident that changes in temp**
       v. unlikely to be natural

Effects of CC
       rise in sea levels
       effs on agriculture
       effs on natural ecosystems (rainforest, coral reefs)

       Kyoto targets were weak: called for 5% reduction in emissions, but 60% needed

       + USA abandoned agreement

Reasons why intern'l action is difficult
1. **science is complex; public misunderstanding – or disinformation**
2. **energy use and agriculture central to mod soc, so diff. to change**
3. **effs mainly felt in dev'ing countries**

Ways to progress?
     can do s.th. as individuals
          take energy-efficiency measures in the home
          use the car less
          buy electricity from companies using renewable energy sources
     intern'l action more problematic.
     not sure how this can happen, but need to realise we are all in same boat / interlinked global econ.

Conclusion
hope that dev'd countries will see imp. of
1. **helping dev'ing countries find clean energy sources**
2. **reducing own emissions – may mean reducing personal consumption**

Final Review Ways of continuing to improve your listening

TONY LYNCH

so now we've come to the end of the *Study Listening* course what I'd like to do / is to look at ways in which you can carry on practising your listening skills / not just in lectures but / more generally too /

firstly I suggest you read as much as you can in English / um this will help you / increase / expand your vocabulary and / in turn that will help you cope better with spoken English /

the second point is linked to the first / I think it's essential to make effective use of the information in your dictionary in your English dictionary on how words are pronounced and stressed / students have told me / how much it helps them to get an accurate idea of how a word sounds / and not just how it's spelt and what it means / because otherwise they may not recognise a word when it's spoken that they know in printed form /

the third point I'd make is that if you're attending an academic course / it's really important to have the confidence to ask / when you haven't understood something / um lecturers will generally leave some time / in Britain usually at the end of the lecture / for you to ask questions / now of course I do know / that many international students don't find it easy to ask that sort of question in public / um because / obviously it shows that you haven't understood / so if you find it hard to speak to the lecturer then I'd say ask another student to explain the point from their notes /

watching TV and listening to the radio can be <u>very</u> good listening practice / not just in English-speaking countries / of course these days it's much easier to catch up with news in English on the Net / particularly useful I think are news programmes / partly because you can

use your background knowledge to understand what's being said / but also because the structure of the news makes understanding easier / what what I mean by structure is that you often hear the first version of a story read out by a newsreader / and then you get a reporter on location somewhere / and then an interview done by the reporter with someone in that location / now in terms of the language that you're… that you hear / the first version from the newsreader will be basically written English read aloud / the reporter will usually speak in a less formal way / probably from notes / and then the interviewee will obviously be speaking spontaneously / and so those three versions get closer and closer to natural speech / and the effect is that the first version helps you understand the second the second helps you understand the third /

uh I'd also like to pass on to you some of the suggestions from international students in Scotland / um there are three on your handout that I want to pick out as particularly interesting / see what you think /

um student number three / talked about using dictation / and how the gaps in your dictation tell you what your listening problems are / this is rather similar to some of the listening that we've done in the troubleshooting activities in this course /

then there's student number eight / um student number eight talked about the fact that there are bigger differences among British people's accents than among foreigners' accents / now what she was saying about native speakers' variation in accent is uh absolutely true / um to show you what I mean / if I ask a class of learners of English to pronounce the word H-O-U-S-E / 'house' / all of them will pronounce the vowel as something like 'ow' / but uh depending where you are in the British Isles you'll hear local people say that word roughly like this (*approximations to 'house' as said in Dublin, Belfast, Manchester, Bristol, London, Newcastle and Edinburgh*) / now I've never heard a foreign student produce that word with as much variety as that / so listening and talking to other learners of English is in fact a very good way of increasing your listening fluency / and of course better preparation in the long term for listening to English in an international setting /

the last one / number ten / is I think a very interesting suggestion / this was a student from Japan / who played novels and stories on his Walkman / uh as he said quote 'to force my mind to think in English when I'm not reading or writing and speaking' unquote / now what he was trying to do was to make his processing more automatic / and some of the things that we've done in this course have been about paying conscious attention to what you're doing when you're listening / the sort of thing we've done with the macrostrategies / but that also needs to be combined with simply as much exposure to the spoken language as you can get / in order to make your listening more automatic / and so the idea of the need for a balance between conscious attention and plenty of practice is I think a very good note to end on / thank you very much / and good luck with your listening /

WAYS TO IMPROVE LISTENING – not just in lectures

1. read ↗ vocab, which helps

2. make eff. use of dictionary
   Pron. + stress → recognise word when spoken

3. ask Qs
   If not poss. to ask lecturers, ask student

4. TV/radio/net
   news progs useful ∴ structure
   ↓   1. newsreader (written English) ⎤ more
       2. reporter (from notes)   ⎥ like
   ↓   3. interviewee (spontaneous)   ⎦↓ speech

Suggestions from students

student ③ dictation – like 'troubleshooting'

 " " ⑧ wide range of accents in B.Isles, so
           talking to other foreign students is good
           practice and prep. for listening to intern'l Eng.

 " " ⑩ make listening more automatic

▷ in "study listening" ⟨ conscious attention (m'strategies)
                         ⟨ exposure/practice

need a balance betw. conscious attention + practice

Teaching notes

I hope you will find these Notes a help, rather than a hindrance. I have tried to make them concise but not so brief that they are obscure. In some cases, the 'answers' I provide are correct answers to single-solution questions, but in many cases they are my suggestions only. In some places I have outlined how I would approach a task with my students in Edinburgh. You may prefer to teach the materials differently to suit your class, especially the short reading and pre-listening vocabulary activities.

I hope you will enjoy using these materials. If you would like to contact me with comments or suggestions, my email address is A.J.Lynch@ed.ac.uk

Tony Lynch
Edinburgh
Scotland

Introduction **Two functions of listening**

PRE-LISTENING

This first lesson is intended, in particular, to allow students to share their experiences of lectures (pages 10–11) and of note-taking techniques (12–14). If you are teaching a class to whom lecture listening and taking notes are new, then you could spend more time on the techniques section.

In **Defining a lecture, Your experience of lectures** and **Lecturing styles**, I have tried to allow for differences in cultural patterns around the academic world. When the text says 'in your country', you can adapt that to mean the students' home country or the place where they are currently studying with you. You can highlight and discuss issues such as the 'normal' length of lectures (page 10) or lecturers' style of presentation (page 11). The three-way classification of lecturing styles comes originally from a paper by Dudley-Evans and Johns (1981); details are in the References at the end of the book.

Difficulties in lectures

2 a) *Physical setting* – size and acoustics of the room; distance between student and lecturer; background noise from outside; and noises inside the room (air conditioning, coughing, moving chairs, etc.).

   b) *Speaker* – accent; lack of clarity of delivery (mumbling, hesitations, etc.); speed of speaking, especially lack of adequate pauses; lecturing style (a scripted lecture is usually harder for listeners to follow than one based on brief notes).

   c) *Subject* – unfamiliarity; lack of interest or relevance for the listener; complexity or abstractness of the topic.

   d) *Language* – use of colloquial English (e.g. '*the long and the short of it is …*' or '*what this boils down to …*': to mean *in essence*); technical vocabulary, or familiar vocabulary used in an unfamiliar way; foreign expressions (especially Latin and French in academic English).

Effective lecturing

Speaking techniques – using list markers for a series of related points; clearly signalling a move to a new topic; involving the audience by encouraging them to ask questions; speaking slower on key points; asking the audience questions.

Technology – showing key words in written form (on the board, OHP or computer display); using diagrams and graphics to show interrelationships and change; providing fill-in handouts or notes for students to take away.

Spoken and written language

1 The main reason for the differences in spoken and written language is the difference in planning time available to speakers and writers. Among the main features of spoken English are:
  - speakers speak in short bursts or chunks
  - spoken English uses more coordination (*and, but, or, so*) than subordination
  - speech has a higher ratio of 'little words' (pronouns, articles, particles, prepositions, the verb *be*, auxiliary verbs, conjunctions) to content words
  - speakers hesitate, make false starts and slips, and change their minds as they are talking; writers are able to edit those things out invisibly
  - spontaneous speech is full of fillers (*um, sort of, like*) and interactive markers (*well, you know, yeah?*)
  - speakers vary in speed and accent
  - speech gets greater support from visual element (teaching aids; paralanguage).

2 [Open questions] Most students prefer reading to listening, citing problems stemming from the real-time nature of listening, as opposed to the more time-manageable activity of reading. Exceptions are particular time-pressured situations such as reading film subtitles – or lecturers' overheads!

Reading a full script results in fewer pauses, and of course fewer hesitations and changes of mind. The text itself is normally closer to written language, which tends to be denser in information and therefore harder to understand from listening.

Listening

Answer: 1a). I worked from a sort of 'script' – a transcript of a talk I had given working from brief notes.

Note-taking techniques

1 Notes should be a selective summary of main points and not an exact copy.
2 Notes remind us of what someone has said. They may have a short-term or long-term purpose. In an academic context, notes can serve as revision material for exams, or as support material for written assignments.
3 Normally they're written solely for the note-taker.

Rule 1: Be selective

The quantity of notes depends partly on individual preference and the ability to write (re-code) fast, but mainly on knowledge of the topic. So I'd expect the postgraduate to make fewer notes, assuming they knew more about the topic and therefore had less need to make full notes.

Rule 2: Be brief

1. a) *exempli gratia* = for example
   b) *Nota Bene* = (note well) bear in mind
   c) *id est* = that is
   d) *et cetera* = (and the rest) and so on
   e) *confere* = compare this with
   f) *vice versa* = the other way round.
2. a) International Labour Office (or Organisation)
   b) World Health Organisation
   c) Organisation of Petroleum Exporting Countries
   d) Australian Broadcasting Corporation
   e) United Nations Education Scientific and Cultural Organisation.
3. a)–h) In my own notes, these abbreviations mean *important*, *but*, *international*, *essential*, *future*, *estimated*, *problem* or *probable*, and *student*.

	Symbol	Meaning
a)	=	'is the same as'
b)	+	'in addition'
c)	→	'causes' or 'leads to' or 'results in'
d)	??	'not clear to me' or 'is that true?'
e)	>	'is greater than'
f)	!	'important point'
g)	↑	'grows', 'rises', or 'raises'
h)	←	'is caused by', 'results from'
i)	≈	'varies with' or 'changes according to'

Rule 3: Be clear

Personally, I take linear notes when I'm listening (or reading), but I make mind maps when I'm planning to write something or to give a talk. The use of mind maps seems to be spreading; I usually find that at least one person in a class uses them when listening to lectures.

LISTENING

Listening and note-taking and Comparing notes

My talk is short and relatively straightforward, so I haven't provided a note-frame. Units 1–8 include an optional note-frame or handout. If your class have not done note-taking before, then you may want to play the talk twice.

Macrostrategies

The final section is a pointer to the way the course develops. If your students have not read the *To the student* section, now is a good time to do that and to study the *Course Map*. Encourage them to ask questions about the course at this stage.

If your students have found the technical side of the note-taking in this unit difficult, I suggest you give them more practice on two or three short note-based talks before moving on to Unit 1. The talks should not be complex; a set of reasons for doing something, or a set of problems with some aspect of language learning, would be suitable material.

Unit 1 Problems of urbanisation

Macrostrategy 1: Predicting

When introducing the notion of predicting you could use the example below to get your students to predict what is likely to be said in that situation.

Example: *A woman out shopping loses a wallet or purse containing money, credit cards and documents. She goes to a police station to report what has happened. The police officer listens to the story and then says, 'Well, I have some good news and some bad news for you.'*

Ask your students what they think the police officer will say next.

PRE-LISTENING

Introduction to the lecture topic: Urbanisation

This section in each unit is intended to be a quick preparation for the listening to come. The reading texts I have chosen should stimulate the students to recall relevant background knowledge and to highlight the necessary vocabulary. If you think your students will find a particular text difficult, then you could omit it and move straight to the Content questions.

Reading

1–2 My choice is the second sentence in the first paragraph. 'One of the greatest problems…'.

3 Two million was Schumacher's estimate of the number of villages in the developing world.

Pre-listening discussion: Content

1–4 [Open answers] Ask the students to discuss the questions in small groups, allowing 60–90 seconds for each one and then getting their answers. I write up the groups' answers to questions 3 and 4, to refer to later.

Pre-listening discussion: Language

These words may be unfamiliar, but encourage the students to guess at their meanings from their form. If you have a monolingual class, then of course you can ask them to translate the words. But get them to talk about their predictions in English, to foreground the relevant vocabulary.

The lecturer

Canadian and northern US accents are very similar; many speakers from those regions can find it hard to distinguish them. On pages 128–129 is an *Accent summary*, in case you want to point out to your students the main distinctive features of the lecturers' accents. The words listed on pages 128–129 were used by the lecturer in question, in the opening or closing section of their lecture. The words are also shown in grey type in *Transcripts and sample notes*.

Lecture language: Signpost markers

Ask the students to suggest other expressions to add to those in the boxes. Here – and elsewhere – I have used the IELTS box to show that a task is similar to one found in the IELTS test or practises a skill relevant to the test.

Lecture language: List markers

the first	the second	the third	...	the last the final
one	two	three	...	last
firstly**	secondly	thirdly	...	lastly finally
first	then	then next	...	lastly finally
one	another	another a further ...	...	the last

**In British English *firstly*, *secondly* etc. are used for items in a list, e.g reasons, but not to mark time order. *First, second* etc. can be used for items in a list and also for time order.

FIRST LISTENING

Listening and note-taking

Get the students to recall and review their earlier predictions about what the lecturer would mention. Play the first 4 minutes or so, as far as the start of the final *policies* section, including the opening sentence '*Now I'd like to move on to three possible policies…*' and then stop the tape. Ask them to predict what those three policies are going to be. Spend a short time (1–2 minutes) getting predictions from the class, then play the final section.

Oral summary

The aim here is to provide brief student–student interaction before they listen again to the lecture. Listen in on the pairs' talk to assess how well they have done and where the main problems lie.

SECOND LISTENING

Detailed note-taking and Comparing notes

If the class seems to have understood the lecture well on first hearing, omit this stage. Most classes will need the second listening, though. Once that is completed, get the students to compare their notes with each other's and then with the sample notes on page 135.

AFTER LISTENING
Post-listening: Focus on language

The answers to all the Focus on Language tasks for each unit are marked in some way (according to the instructions) in the relevant full transcript in *Transcript and sample notes*. The ones for this unit are on pages 134–135.

Post-listening: Focus on content
Discussion and reaction and *Critical thinking*

[Open answers] For question 1, you can refer students back to the predictions they made earlier. Check off (tick) those they predicted correctly.

Optional follow-up: Writing

Although the primary focus of this course is listening, some students may want to write to make active use of the language and ideas they have encountered in the lecture. The task here is similar to an IELTS Writing task 2 (essay).

As an alternative, they could write a summary of Adrienne Hunter's talk. If so, I'd ask them to base it on their notes, not the transcript. (They will not get the chance to use transcripts in real life, but they will need to work from notes when writing essays and other assignments.)

Unit 2 Differences between academic cultures
Macrostrategy 2: Monitoring

Below is the text to practise monitoring. It contains a number of problem points – underlined in the text – that will require the students to monitor carefully in order to make sense of them. Ask the students to take notes as you read them the text.

A lot of universities now run English language courses for international students. In some cases students attend the courses before they start their degrees and in others they do them after they have already begun a degree. These two types of course are called in-session and pre-session courses.

One snag with in-session courses is that the students who would probably benefit most from them are those who are weakest in English, but because of their language level those are also the students that find their subject courses difficult, so they have to spend extra time on their course work, especially reading. So they have less time to spend on their English classes.

Probably the most important language skill for students to work on is listening. Most people believe it's the key to success, particularly in the early part of a lecture-based degree. Students who find it hard to understand their lectures tend to fall behind the others and it's <u>very easy</u> to get into a situation where you can't catch up again. So one way that universities can help is by running intensive listening classes, especially in the last few days before the academic year. But rather than <u>putting all their eggs into that particular basket</u>, what universities should really also be doing is training their lecturers to teach international classes and to make their lectures simpler to follow. There are a number of things lecturers can do to help make it easier for international students to understand what they're saying, such as …

<u>Pause here</u> and ask the students to predict what's coming. Get them to predict as precisely as possible – specific 'things' a lecturer can do. After small group discussion, collect and write up their suggestions. Then read out the last part of the original text:

…speaking more slowly and more clearly, encouraging questions from the students, improving their use of visual materials and using signpost markers to make clear the structure of their lecture.

Here are some comments on the problem points in the text.
- '*in-session and pre-session*' should have been the other way round, to match the preceding descriptions of the two types of course
- if the word '*snag*' is unfamiliar, the listener needs to monitor for clues as to whether it's positive or negative
- at first, the students may think that '*very easy*' contradicts the idea of a problem, but this is then resolved by the fact that it refers to the fact that 'you can't catch up again'
- idioms like '*putting all your eggs in one basket*' – which are common in speech – require careful attention on the listener's part to the meaning clues around them.

PRE-LISTENING

Introduction to the lecture topic: Academic cultures
Reading
If you want to use a specific example of something taken for granted in an academic culture, ask what happens if a student hands an essay in late – whether it's tolerated, accepted, penalised, etc.

Pre-listening discussion: Content

[Open answers] The last question is meant to set the students up for the talk they are about to hear.

Pre-listening discussion: Language

Check that they understand that *Pride comes before a fall* has a negative meaning in English and is a sort of warning. Some students interpret the word pride positively – 'being proud of what you do' – and interpret the proverb as meaning something like 'Taking pride in what you do is more important than (worrying about) failing'.

The lecturer

For the main features of a New Zealand accent, see the *Accent summary* on page 128.

Lecture language: Quotations and Drawing conclusions

Again, you could elicit further examples of the expressions for quoting and concluding – e.g. *what we should take from this* and *the thing to remember about this* …

FIRST/SECOND LISTENING

The note-frame does not show the number of points that Olwyn Alexander mentions when she talks at the end about the lesson she learnt from the experience, because that issue is featured in **Comparing notes**.

AFTER LISTENING

Post-listening: Focus on language

1–4 [Answer checking delayed] The four meanings of 'or' are picked up in the **transcript listening** that follows.

Fast speech

This is a brief introduction to an important area of the listening process. I have included just a small set of examples here, because we come back to the recognition of rapid speech in later units.

One additional example of **assimilation** you might try on your students is *How to recognise speech*. When said naturally, it can sound exactly the same as *How to wreck a nice beach*. (This is a classic example among Artificial Intelligence researchers interested in speech recognition, for obvious reasons.) However, lower-level learners of English are likely to hear it only as *How to recognise speech* because they may well not know the verb *wreck*.

Reduction is probably the greater source of difficulty for our students. Reduction also makes different words sound the same: in my southern English accent, for example, I'd make no distinction between *she's going to see <u>her</u> doctor* and *she's going to see <u>a</u> doctor*. And in all accents of English, the fact that both *would* and *had* are naturally reduced to *'d* means that *I'd put it on the table* is ambiguous, out of context.

Transcript listening

Stop the tape immediately after each gap, to check what the students have heard. I ask them first to tell me how many words there were [missing from the gap], and then ask them to check the words with their neighbour. Then play the gapped part again and 'compile' the missing words on the board. I find that, between them, a group of students have often identified the individual bits but that no-one got the whole expression on first hearing.

In the case of the 'or' expressions, I ask the students to identify which function of 'or' the speaker was using.

Post-listening: Focus on content

1 Olwyn's move was horizontal, from a postgraduate Dip TEFL course in New Zealand to a Master's course in Britain. She emphasises that from the student's perspective the courses were basically the same.
2 Presumably the diagonal move is the most problematic. There is an interesting and much-quoted paper on this 'double cultural shift' by Brigid Ballard (Ballard 1984).
3 British students also often don't know what to call their lecturers, but seem to worry less about it. I assume that for non-native speakers of English the situation is worse because they may be used to marking respect in their first language by choosing the appropriate form of 'you', whereas in English they don't have that possibility and so addressing a lecturer just as 'you' feels abrupt and over-direct.
4 You should get interesting suggestions. Among those I've had from students are that students ought to stand up when the lecturer enters the lecture theatre, and that they should wait in the room until the lecturer has left.

Critical thinking

Arguably, Olwyn did object, but only indirectly by ironically referring to Pope and Lamb. But she didn't make a formal objection.

This question is intended to lead on to thinking about wider issues of students' status and rights, for example, in a situation where they think a mark they have received is unfair. If you are teaching in an ESL setting, you can get students to discuss the local rules (as far as they are aware of them) for objecting to a mark on a university assignment. In Britain, this leads on to discussing the role of the external examiner, in the case of postgraduate courses.

The second set of questions raises an issue that underlies a great deal of EAP teaching.

1 The answer is (a).
2 In the paragraphs on Western academic reports: *very wordy* and *irrelevant quotations*. There are no negative words in the paragraph on Chinese writing.
3 [Open answers]
4 This question easily spreads into other areas related to writing up research. You may find useful material on the points the students raise in *Study Writing* (see *References* for details).

Unit 3 Teleworking and distance learning
Macrostrategy 3: Responding

I like to give students immediate practice in responding to a short argumentative text, like the one below. It's about whether children find language learning easier than adults do – a topic that most students have very definite views about, as well as being one they've experienced at first hand.

Some people think that the best time to begin studying a foreign language is in childhood, and that the younger you are, the easier it is to learn another language. But there is little evidence that children learning foreign languages at school are any better than adults (people over age 15) in similar classroom situations.

In fact, adults have many advantages over children, such as: better memories, more efficient ways of organising information, longer attention spans, better study habits, and greater ability to do complex mental tasks. Adults are also often better motivated than children: they see learning a foreign language as necessary for their education or career. In addition, adults are particularly sensitive to correctness of grammar and appropriateness of vocabulary – two things that receive attention in most language classrooms.

adapted from Rubin and Thompson (1982: 4)

After reading them the text, I ask the three questions shown on page 37 (slightly rephrased):

* Do you accept that these points are true?
* Can you think of examples that go against the ideas here?

- Do you think that the writer's opinion is reasonable?

The next paragraph of the original text puts forward some opposing points, which you can suggest if your students don't come up with them:

> But age does have some disadvantages. For instance, adults usually want to learn a foreign language in a hurry. Children can devote more time to mastering a language. Also, adults have more complex communication needs, which go beyond just being able to hold a simple conversation.

PRE-LISTENING

Introduction to the lecture topic: Teleworking and distance learning

The original words missing from the five sentences were: 1 'isolated' and 'team'; 2 'uncertain'; 3 'Misunderstandings'; 4 'longer' and 'turn off'; and 5 'resentful'. You can accept any alternatives that are semantically acceptable, e.g. 'envious' instead of 'resentful'.

Pre-listening discussion: Content

1–3 These questions are intended to get the students both predicting the issues that will be raised in the lecture and also giving their responses to those points in advance. Compile the pros and cons on the board, to compare later with what the lecturer actually says. Q1 is meant to balance the negative points mentioned in the five sentences the students have discussed under *Introduction to the topic.*

Pre-listening discussion: Language

1 Alternative terms mentioned in the lecture: *e-working, telecommuting* and *telestudying.*
2 We also talk about *pluses and minuses,* and *negatives and positives* (as nouns). Other negative words are *snag* and *drawback* (the latter is used in the lecture).

The lecturer

The main distinguishing features of Australian vowels are shown in the *Accent summary* on page 128. The distinctive words listed, from the opening three sections of his lecture, are shown in shading on page 139. Ron Howard's Australian accent is quite slight, because he has worked for many years in Britain.

Lecture language: Importance markers and Definitions and explanations

You may want to ask the students to come up with further expressions they have heard for these language functions. I also encourage my students to add to these (and the other) language lists any useful expressions they notice later in the course.

FIRST LISTENING
Listening and note-taking
Highlight the two **Responding** questions 2a and 2b on page 40 before playing the talk.

Oral summary
This particular talk has a clear pros-and-cons structure, which is reflected in the note-frame. I get one partner in each pair to summarise the advantages and the other the disadvantages.

SECOND LISTENING
Detailed note-taking
Before playing the lecture again, check whether they've spotted the points that Ron Howard marked as more important. If so, ask whether and how they've shown this in their notes. Compare and discuss alternative ways of doing this before they listen the second time.

AFTER LISTENING
Troubleshooting
The main difficulty that my students have encountered is the relative absence of list markers. So I replay the talk, section by section, getting them to check the number of points they've identified in each.

Then they can compare their answers to the *lecturer's* notes, made to refer to as he was speaking. So there could be interesting differences between these and the notes of *listeners*, who need to reflect the lecturer's comments on relative importance of advantages. That is not shown in his notes to himself.

Post-listening: Focus on language

1 [Transcript listening] I have used asterisks in the transcript to show the places where I stop the tape to check students' understanding. But if your class has had no great difficulty with the first two stages of listening and note-taking, you could play the tape straight through.

2 Answers are marked in the usual way in the transcript on pages 139–141.

Post-listening: Focus on content
Responding and Discussion

[Open answers] These questions are meant to draw students' attention to the Responding macrostrategy. Teleworking and distance learning are things that many students now have personal experience of, and I've found no problem in getting my classes to add to, and to question, the points raised in the talk.

Role-play

This gives the class the chance to practise using the vocabulary and the ideas they've heard Ron Howard talk about.

Optional follow-up: Writing

If the abrupt start of Ron's lecture didn't cause any problems for your students, then you could omit this task. But it does allow you scope for focusing again on the stylistic differences between speech and writing, discussed earlier in the Introduction unit.

Unit 4 Language strategies for awkward situations
Macrostrategy 4: Clarifying

It's hard to overestimate the value of Clarifying in foreign language listening. One recent article (Ridgway 2000) even claimed it is the only listening strategy that language learners need – although that was for conversational listening, rather than listening to academic lectures.

In a typical lecture there is very limited time for students to ask questions, which certainly makes it more difficult for them to get their doubts cleared up. That makes it even more important that students focus on the key points that are unclear in their understanding of what a lecturer has said.

1–3 Of course, there are also cultural factors at play in asking lecturers questions in public, which are explored in the three discussion points at the start of the unit. The third question, in particular, can lead to animated discussion of the rights and responsibilities in the student–lecturer relationship.

Clarifying expressions

In my experience students tend to use the verbs *catch* and *get* interchangeably when asking for clarification. The usage shown in the list of expressions reflects what you hear in Britain and, I think, other English-speaking countries: *catch* meaning *hear*, and *get* meaning *understand*. If this is different from the way they are used in your context, point that out.

PRE-LISTENING

Introduction to the lecture topic: Language strategies for awkward situations

You may have first-hand experience of the differences between British and other English-speaking cultures in this area of directness. I am assured by American colleagues that they would only use *Could you possibly…* to express extreme sarcasm. In Britain it is considered a very polite – possibly over-polite – request.

Pre-listening discussion: Content

1–12 You may need to limit the time on discussion here! I find this list generates a great deal of argument. Stress that more than one of the 12 responses can be appropriate. If your class includes students from different cultures, they may find it hard to agree on what counts as appropriate in English, or rather in the relevant English-speaking culture.

I ask my students what they themselves would say to the shop assistant in that situation. My own usual response is a mixture of numbers 4 and 7 – *I'm just looking, thanks.*

Pre-listening discussion: Language

Check that the students know the meanings of the military terms and the animals.

Expressions of contrast

As usual, ask for additional expressions of the same type. Students will sometimes suggest *It is not only (X), it's also (Y)*. However, that marks <u>addition</u> rather than contrast.

If the students suggest '*on the contrary*' as an expression of contrast, point out that, in conversation, it is only used to <u>counter</u> what the other person has just suggested.

A: *I suppose you're glad she's resigned.*
B: *On the contrary. I'm rather disappointed.*

When used in writing or a lecture, it is used to emphasise or extend a negative point.

> Interpreting abstract art is not easy. On the contrary, it is extremely complex.

The lecturer

Hugh Trappes-Lomax's accent is Received Pronunciation (RP), which many people outside Britain still think of as the British accent. For its main features, see the *Accents summary* on page 128. The words listed are shown in shading in the transcript on page 143.

Exploiting the information in a handout

Allow plenty of time for the students to study the handout carefully, for two reasons. Firstly, it contains some probably unfamiliar vocabulary and detailed visual clues. Secondly, Hugh Trappes-Lomax speaks relatively quickly, and they will need to complete the handout at speed.

1 They are terms being defined.
2 Single quotation marks = quotations from a written source; double = examples.
3 Indentation is used to show the relationship between points and sub-points, e.g. the various categories and sub-categories of euphemism.

FIRST LISTENING

Listening and note-taking

Remind the class about the Clarifying macrostrategy. Ask them how they plan to show on their handout the points where they want/need to ask a clarifying question.

Comparing notes

At this stage, encourage the students to answer each other's clarifying questions. Don't yet confirm or reject their answers, though, because the second listening is intended to focus on points for clarification.

AFTER LISTENING

Post-listening: Focus on language

Clarifying

At each stopping point, get the students to ask clarifying questions they feel are necessary. Answer them yourself or leave it to other students to do this.

Troubleshooting

One likely difficulty is the relative lack of redundancy and repetition. However, I stress the way they (should) have been able to use the very full information in the handout to compensate for the lack of repetition.

The students may say, after they've seen the transcript, that the lecturer used a lot of words they didn't know. If so, I'd point out that, in this case, the target was for them to be able to complete the handout. To do that, you don't need to have understood every word.

The *Recognising stressed words* exercise helps students cope with fluent speech. You could treat this as a straightforward listening task – listening and marking up the transcript and then comparing their answers. Alternatively, you could ask the students to read the transcript to themselves and mark the words that they predict the speaker will stress, before you play the tape again for them to check their predictions. Choose whichever you think will suit the level of your class.

Post-listening: Focus on content

Discussion: Politeness and tact

I think you'll find plenty of mileage in these questions.

1 This quesion is designed for classes in which the students have different first languages, but the second point – on deciding which pronoun to use – can be discussed successfully even when the students share the same language.

2 In my case, I get called 'sir' in some shops in Britain. I don't think I call anybody 'madam', 'miss' or 'sir' now, though I do remember that students still called tutors 'sir' at Cambridge in the early 1970s.

3 Again, I find that this question of loss of face on the part of lecturer or student provokes quite extensive discussion, especially among students from East Asia, who are aware of different conventions applying in the country where they are studying or intending to study.

Optional: Political correctness

At the time of writing (2003) political correctness still arouses considerable public interest and debate in Britain. If it's not relevant in your teaching situation, omit this section. As you've heard, Hugh Trappes-Lomax was in favour of some PC expressions, but not when taken to extremes.

Unit 5 Targets for preventive medicine
Macrostrategy 5: Inferencing

The vital thing in these three tasks is to create a positive attitude to guessing. In my experience, many students – in particular, from Asian cultures – can be reluctant to guess, or at least to admit they have guessed. They may even feel that guessing is somehow 'cheating'. So the aim here is to encourage students to guess and to get them to explain the reasons behind their guesses. I think learners very rarely just guess; they use all sorts of reasonable clues.

Guessing from incomplete information

Here's the mini-story for you to read aloud to the class:

When I first went into the System, I had to queue for ages. At first the woman did not understand what I had asked her for, but eventually she found the bottles I wanted. Then, just as I was about to pay, the red light went on. So it was a good thing I had my passport with me.

Most people guess the events take place in the duty-free shop at an airport or ferry terminal (*queue, bottles, passport*). They may also guess that it must be in a foreign country (as the *woman didn't understand* me). If that's what your students think, ask them to explain what the red light was for.

And what about the passport? If it had been a duty-free airport shop, then surely I would have had to show a boarding pass, rather than a passport.

You could also tell them that the word System has a capital S, not a small S, but that may not add very much to help them.

The mini-story describes what happened to me regularly in Sweden when I was teaching English there in the early 1970s. In those days you could only buy wine and spirits from a shop owned by the government monopoly Systembolaget, popularly shortened to Systemet (or 'the System'). The layout of the shops was like a bank, so the customers had no access to the bottles; you gave your order to an assistant, who would fetch the goods you wanted from shelves behind the counter.

Nobody under the age of 21 was allowed to buy goods from Systemet, and if – as I evidently did – you looked younger, the assistant could press a button on the floor with her foot. This made a red light on the top of her cash register come on, and when the light came on the customer had to show identification to prove their age. As a foreigner, I didn't have an identity card so I used my passport instead. Swedes tell me that the System has now changed. So you should still be able to use this text as a platform for guessing, even if you have Swedish students in your class!

Guessing at unfamiliar words

The four words are: *a hot-box*; *an undertrial*; *a fire-boy* and the verb *to prepone*.

Read them out for the students to write down. Don't tell them (yet) how to spell the words, because an essential micro-skill is the ability to guess at an English word's spelling from its sound. These words should be relatively easy to get right.

Get the students to work on the words in small groups. When they have had time to work out their guesses, ask them to put the words in order of confidence – i.e. how sure the students are that they are correct. Most confident = 1; least confident = 4.

The four words are all in use in India. Answers:

- *a hot-box* is a metal container in which people take their lunch to work, to keep it warm
- *an undertrial* is a defendant in a court case
- *a fire-boy* is a (usually elderly) servant who lights and looks after the coal fires in Himalayan hotels in the winter
- *to prepone* is to bring (a meeting) forward, i.e. the opposite of *to postpone*.

Familiar words, unfamiliar meanings?

Read out two speaking turns at a time – one from Gus and one from Sue – and then stop to give the students time to write down the topic and the clue.

Gus: What's it like then?
Sue: Not bad. It's got a good short menu, which saves quite a bit of time.
STOP 1
Gus: It doesn't have a mouse, does it?
Sue: No, not at that price.
STOP 2
Gus: Anything else special?
Sue: Well, it's got a thing to stop you having to worry about widows and orphans.

STOP 3

Gus: So you're happy with it, then?

Sue: So far, yes.

STOP 4

Gus: And did you get the 512 in the end?

Sue: No the 256.

END

Some students will guess (correctly) at Stop 1 that Gus and Sue are talking about a new computer, but then they may have doubts at Stop 3. Most students start by guessing it's about a restaurant, and at Stop 2 think that an expensive restaurant wouldn't have mice. But they also have doubts by Stop 3. A few students may even write down five different topics at the five stopping points. If you're interested, there's a discussion of interpretations of the conversation in Lynch 1996: 89–91.

PRE-LISTENING

Introduction to the lecture topic: Targets for preventive medicine

Ask the students what the equivalent is for the proverb in their first languages. When they have discussed 1–3, check whether they need you to explain any of the words from the text.

Pre-listening discussion: Content

These questions should help students to call up relevant background knowledge and to predict the likely content of the lecture. The use of the terms *developing* and *developed* to refer to countries at different stages of economic development can be controversial, and is discussed later in the unit.

Pre-listening discussion: Language

Work through the list and elicit explanations from the class. Give them help only if they ask for it.

The lecturer

For comments on the common features of Scottish accents, see the *Accent summary* on page 129. Like other Scots, Eric Glendinning sounds all 'r's'. In his case, he pronounces 'r' as a longitudinal approximant, rather like most North Americans. In other Scottish accents, 'r' is trilled ('rolled'). The words listed in the summary are shown in shading in the transcript on page 148.

Lecture language: Stress on key words

In the original sentences, taken from the first edition of the book, the words stressed were:

1 *choose – fuel – food*
2 *possibility – developing – greater – developed*
3 *two – three – even one*

Lecture language: Fast speech

To illustrate this point, you need to read the extract aloud to the students. Make sure you read the 'although' clause in smaller font much faster and more quietly than the other parts.

For this point and the next, on **Recycling**, you could take the opportunity to make the point (again) that students shouldn't be aiming for 100% comprehension. In my experience, listeners can manage if they understand 70–75% of a lecture – provided, of course, that they identify the key points.

FIRST LISTENING

Take a minute or two to review the **Inferencing** macrostrategy and the sources of potential help – sounds, subject knowledge and context.

Read out the note on page 66 telling them that you are going to cover the sound of some of the words in the lecture. The words that I cover up are shown in boxes in transcript sections 2–5 in this unit, so you can use that as your 'script' for when to add sound effects while the students are listening and taking notes. The words chosen are ones that are guessable from their context.

When you reach those points in the lecture recording, make a suitable noise (e.g. cough, sneeze or bang a book shut), so the students can't hear the word. Alternatively, turn the volume down *briefly* to zero.

This is intended to reflect the coughing, banging of doors and so on that listeners have to put up with in real lectures. The point is to persuade students that we can guess – sometimes exactly, sometimes approximately – at words we can't actually hear.

At the end of the first listening, ask the students what their guesses were. Discuss with them how plausible or acceptable their guesses are.

section	actual word	acceptable alternatives
2	doubled	risen, increased, gone up
3	soap	?
4	behaviour	lifestyle, habits
5	kill (the mosquitoes) drugs stomachs	exterminate, get rid of tablets, pills, medicine? ?

SECOND LISTENING

Get them to review their notes after their oral summary. Which parts of the lecture do they need to pay particular attention to?

Comparing notes

Have they identified the point of the two case histories? Sometimes students get the details but not the overall point.

AFTER LISTENING

Troubleshooting

The problematic expression that includes *refrigerated ships* has been left blank in section 3 of the transcript to encourage discussion as to what Eric Glendinning actually said.

The answers to the various tasks are underlined in the full transcript on pages 148–150.

In sections 4 and 5, where the students are asked to guess at meanings, it is worth spending some time comparing and 'deconstructing' the mental routes to their guesses. Here, for example, are some of the meanings of *outstripped* that my students have suggested, after being given the word out of context:

lost, exposed, out-of-date, excluded, redecorated, confused, beaten, excellent

You can see how some guesses have been based on the prefix 'out-', and others on 'strip' or 'stripe'. Again, it's important – as well as interesting – to get the students to explain how they reached their interpretation.

at the end of the day = in the end; ultimately; when you have taken everything into account

for my money = in my view; for me

Post-listening: Focus on content

As before, the open questions in this section are meant to require different types of listener response.

You may want to spend more time on the **Critical thinking** questions if your students are unhappy with the common use of terms like *developing, underdeveloped, low-income, Third World* and *South*.

Unit 6 Cloning: The significance of Dolly

This lecture is rather more technical than the others, in the sense that it contains a higher proportion of specific terms – for details, see *Appendix: Vocabulary in academic listening* on page 213.
I have designed the pre-listening and listening tasks with that extra difficulty in mind. If you think that it would be too difficult to use the unit as it stands, here are various alternatives.

- Give your students the first half of the note-frame (page 80 or 81) already completed. Start the listening at the section beginning '*Most of the public fascination…*' on page 86. The second half seems less technical than the first.
- Ask the students to look through the 'off-list' words from the lecture as homework before the class – see page 213.
- Choose which of the off-list words you want to pre-teach or highlight in class before listening.
- Get the students to read the transcript as they listen and make notes.
- Reverse the normal order of tasks in this unit. Do the **Focus on Language** tasks (pages 83–89, or 86–89) first, and then the **Note-taking** (page 79–80).
- If necessary, you could omit this unit altogether. However, teachers using the book in Edinburgh and elsewhere have reported that their students – primarily postgraduates, but not necessarily from the life sciences – have been able to use the unit as it stands.

Macrostrategy 6: Evaluating

'Internal' listener factors that my students have cited: tiredness, boredom, believing that a topic is irrelevant to them, irritation at their neighbour's gum-chewing, thinking about something else.

Evaluating your listening

Allow plenty of time for the students to work in groups on this, if it's something they haven't really thought about before. Get 'reporters' to summarise the groups' discussions. The questions are designed to get gradually more specific, which is meant to help the students prepare for the cloning lecture – i.e. evaluating themselves against a realistic target, rather than believing they need to achieve 100% understanding.

Pre-listening

Introduction to the lecture topic: Genetic research and cloning

Reading

I'd ask the students to prepare this text at home before the listening class. It contains more technical terms than the other readings in the book, but provides the background necessary to make sense of the lecture.

Pre-listening discussion: Content

The idea here is that the students should use what they already know about cloning in general and Dolly in particular. So the definitions of *clone* should come from their heads rather than from a dictionary.

Elicit the answers and compile them on the board for later comparison. Don't confirm or reject any answers yet, but encourage suggestions.

Pre-listening discussion: Language

I've chosen terms that I expect to be unfamiliar to my students, unless they are studying in a bio-medical field. Only *xenotransplantation* is actually essential for effective note-taking.

The lecturer

Harry Griffin is originally from a part of Lancashire (Blackburn) where people pronounce all 'r's, for example in words like *organ* and *part*. For the main features of northern English accents, see the *Accent summary* on page 129. The words listed in the summary are shown in shading in the transcript on page 153.

FIRST LISTENING

Get the students to talk about the merits of the two types of note-frame. Which do they prefer and why? Which one do they think is easier to use? Which one is more like a lecture handout?

Play the tape once and then move straight to the **Evaluating your listening** task on page 82. The aim is for the students to assess their own success in comprehension *before* comparing their notes with someone else. When they have compared notes, ask them to look back to the evaluation answers they gave to the questions on page 77. You may find that they have under-estimated their listening; that's certainly what many of my students do. If so, they should then be encouraged when they do the note comparison task at the end of the Evaluating section.

SECOND LISTENING

After the second listening, ask the students to share the clarifying questions they individually want to ask. If there are biomedical specialists in the class, they can clarify any doubts that have arisen.

AFTER LISTENING
Post-listening: Focus on language

Section 1
Harry Griffin adds 'or perhaps hasn't developed', which seems to me to be hedging rather than self-correction.

Section 2
There are four steps, as shown in the sample notes. Harry Griffin could have used **next** or **then** (… *this reconstructed embryo* …), and **finally** or **lastly** (*in a small proportion of cases* …).

He stressed <u>*only ONE*</u>, to highlight the very low success rate of cloning – one pregnancy from research work involving a total of 400 eggs.

Section 3
1 Answers are shown in the full transcript.
2 *make it to term* = survive to birth.

Section 4
The problems are shown on the full transcript. The words *up* and *lungs* are pronounced by northern English speakers with a short /u/, as in cook. *After* and *span* are pronounced with a vowel like /ʌ/, as in the word *luck*.

There has been questions raised about … is a grammatical slip (singular *has* instead of plural *have*) of the sort that occurs in natural speech, even of highly educated speakers of English.

Section 5
boil down to = 'are basically' or 'can be summarised as'

into the enucleated oocyte – I have included this as an example where the technical nature of the vocabulary can make it hard even for native listeners to identify the words. I use it to encourage, rather than depress, my students by showing them that native listeners are in the same boat as them when it comes to having to guess.

To do this, I show them the guesses of three of my EFL colleagues in Edinburgh. I had played them this lecture section three times and asked them to fill in the two gaps. Unsurprisingly, all of them were able to identify *boil down to* immediately. Their three attempts at the second gap were:

Anne
1 *into the nucle ... ite*
2 *into the innucl ...*
3 *into the innucleate ... cyte*

Cathy
1 *into the ... nucleated ... site*
2 *into the enucleated um site*
3 *into the enucleated liver??? site*

Michael
1 *into the ?? site*
2 *into the innuclei ? site*
3 *into the inuclei ? site*

most of them have been silenced = 'most of (the genes) have been switched off'

Section 6
Answers are shown boxed in the full transcript. The words 'wholly irresponsible' seem to summarise Harry Griffin's attitude to human cloning.

Section 7
Pauses are marked on the full transcript. Harry Griffin used three expressions to show his opinion of the chances of reviving an extinct species.
• *no chance of success*
• *hopelessly fragmented*
• *simply fanciful*

Section 8
I chose to focus on *we will have either accepted* simply because it is a good illustration of vowel reduction in rapid speech. You can find many other similar examples.

Post-listening: Focus on content and Final evaluation

After the three personal response discussion questions, the **Final evaluation** asks the students to reflect on this unit and then compare their self-assessments. The last question (3) is intended to help you get a firm idea of which aspects of listening or language you should highlight in the final two units, especially as **Troubleshooting** activities.

Unit 7 Measuring quality of life

Integrating the macrostrategies

I usually begin by briefly commenting on the diagram, saying we need to synthesise the six macrostrategies. For example, although we can logically start with (global) **predicting**, as soon as the lecture has started we should be **monitoring**, **inferencing** and **responding**, as well as (locally) **predicting** what's likely to come in the next few seconds, as well as further ahead. Basically, we 'pinball' back and forth among the circles in the diagram.

PRE-LISTENING

Introduction to the lecture topic: Measuring quality of life

The order of importance for the English people interviewed was: money; health; crime; family and friends; job; neighbours and neighbourhood; transportation; housing; environmental problems and pollution; leisure and entertainment; access to open spaces and countryside; education; and religion.

Pre-listening discussion: Language

Answers: 1 *well-being* = definition a); 2 *perception* = e); 3 *index* = f); 4 *holistic* = c); 5 *ranking* = b); 6 *aspiration* and 7 *ambition* are both defined in the CLD as a) [or d)].

My definitions

literacy rate the percentage of a population that is able to read and write

guesstimate a rough calculation of size or number, without adequate evidence

mismatch a situation in which two things (or people) are not equal or suited to each other

league table the colloquial equivalent of *ranking*

The lecturer

It is worth pointing out that, taking a global perspective, there are now probably more non-native speakers than native speakers lecturing in English. (There are certainly more people making daily use of English as an additional language than there are native users.) Many of Mauricéa Lynch's vowels are southern English. Among the non-southern English features of her accent are:

- she tends to pronounce /æ/ as /ʌ/, so that *hat* sounds like *hut.*
- like many Brazilians, she pronounces /l/ at the end of a word, such as *reliable* and *final,* like /-u/, so that the final sounds are roughly /-bu/ and /-nu/. This is in fact also common in parts of Britain, and particularly in Scotland, where she lives.
- with words ending in *–ing* she nasalises the /i/, but does not close the *ng.*

Handout

Explain any terms that are unfamiliar to the students before you play the talk.

Checklist

Use this to review the macrostrategies, including a brief discussion of the Predicting points.

FIRST LISTENING

Follow procedure as set out in **Listening and note-taking**. When they have heard the talk, move straight to **Comparing notes and clarifying**. If there are any points that nobody has understood, answer them yourself or – if you are going to give a second listening – leave it for then, or pick them up when you reach that section in the **Transcript listening**.

SECOND LISTENING

I'd only do this if the majority have found the note-taking difficult.

AFTER LISTENING

Transcript listening

Section 1

In this case the connection among the gaps is that they contain the key content words, so they represent the points that the students should have recognised and noted: *researchers from different fields – psychologists – health service research – vast number of instruments – methodological problems.*

Section 2

Spend 5 minutes or so discussing what the missing words are before playing the tape. The students may be able to use their notes, as well as their language and background knowledge. The answers are marked in the full transcript (pages 158–160).

Section 3

The marker expressions are shown in the full transcript. I think the expression '*no doubt you have your own views*' implies three things: (1) that the speaker has reservations about the Index; (2) that she expects her listeners to share those doubts; and (3) that she is inviting the listeners to comment on those doubts at the end of the lecture. So the link is with the Responding macrostrategy, because the lecturer is encouraging an individual (critical) listener response to the HDI.

Section 4

Answers are shown in the full transcript. After checking them, you could ask the students to underline the points highlighted by the markers.

Section 5

One chain of reference is: *people living in Scotland – the public – the people – people's quality of life – ordinary citizens – their lives.*

The other is: *a small group of decision-makers and influential people – the group – some of them – those who make decisions affecting* (people's quality of life).

The slip of the tongue occurred in the second gap, where Mauricéa Lynch said *disappointed* instead of *disappointing*. As I said in Unit 6, native speakers, too, make slips of this sort. However, an effective listener compensates for slips like these by mentally translating what they hear into what they know the speaker means; they may not even notice a slip, and actually 'hear' it as the intended word.

One very public slip of the tongue that I discuss with my students occurred during the first landing on the moon in 1969. As Neil Armstrong stepped onto the surface, he said 'One small step *for man*. One giant leap for mankind', which is contradictory. He had planned to say 'One small step for *a man*', but in the excitement he got it wrong. You don't get a second chance to be first on the moon, so Armstrong's slip gets repeated every time we see the landing on television.

Section 6

I would choose *we need to be very cautious.*

Post-listening: Focus on content

If your class are interested in following up the talk by reading about quality of life issues, they could try the two websites on the handout. You could also try http://www.defra.gov.uk for an up-to-date picture of attitudes to quality of life in Britain, to compare with those in the 2001 survey.

Critical thinking

Depending on the circumstances in which you are teaching, you could develop these issues into a mini-project. I asked one class in Edinburgh to find something that irritated all of them enough to make them want to write to the city council about it. We discovered they were all offended by the litter outside a fast food restaurant near our institute. The students then composed a very forceful letter, giving plenty of reasons why the council should take action, but in the end decided not to send it. Still, I think they enjoyed the experience of *almost* sending it!

Unit 8 Climate change: Evidence and action

Introduction to the lecture topic: Climate change

The pre-listening **Reading**, **Content** and **Language** activities are meant, as usual, to help foreground what your students know and believe about climate change, prior to taking notes on the lecture.

Pre-listening discussion: Language

The lecturer

For teaching purposes, the accents of the southern English and London lecturers can be considered the same. See the *Accent summary* on page 129. The words listed occurred in the final two sections of Simon Allen's lecture and are in shading in the transcript on page 168.

On page 107 I have suggested the students check the *Academic Word List* keywords featured in the talk. If your class is relatively advanced, you could omit this.

Checklist for integrating the macrostrategies

As for Unit 7. This time you can refer back to the students' self-evaluation at the end of the *Quality of life* lecture, to help highlight the macrostrategies they ought to focus on this time.

FIRST LISTENING

Listening and note-taking

Talk to the students about how they want to make notes on this lecture. Since Simon Allen spoke without using a handout, the most realistic type of listening would be for them to take notes from scratch, using no preparation apart from their discussion of the macrostrategies checklist, i.e. without the advantage of previewing the note-frame headings.

Comparing notes and clarifying

As set out on page 112.

Troubleshooting

The troubleshooting point is one that has come up in my classes. In common with other speakers with a non-rhotic (*r*-less) accent – e.g. from Australia, New Zealand and many parts of England and Wales – Simon Allen pronounces *cause* and *cores* the same. This can be a problem for students who have got used to North American, Irish or Scottish accents. If your students have had no difficulty with *ice cores*, move on to discuss other points they have found problematic.

Transcript listening

This unit has more transcript listening tasks because the lecture itself is longer than the others. In case you don't have time for all of them, I suggest you check which ones you might leave out.

Sections 1 and 2

For answers see the full transcript (pages 164–168). There are four proxy measures: tree rings; banding in corals; lake sediments; and ice cores. The period in question is 420,000 years.

Sections 3 and 4

For answers see the full transcript. *Factored in* = included in the calculation, or taken into account.

Section 5

Simon Allen mentions two factors: (1) the targets set were too low anyway; and (2) the fact that the USA withdrew from the agreement.

Sections 6 and 7
For answers see the full transcript.

Section 8
Chain 1 (developed countries) = *rich industrialised countries – the countries responsible (for the pollution) – the countries (have strong economies)*. Chain 2 (developing countries) = *developing countries – their countries – the people who're going to suffer – people in far away places – future generations – in these countries*.

The word in both gaps is *around*: in the first gap, it meant 'available' and in the second, 'alive'.

Section 9
For answers see the full transcript.

AFTER LISTENING
Post-listening discussion: Focus on content
I have included a variety of questions for discussion and you may want to select from those listed. If you have students who are specialists in earth sciences, you could ask them to act as a panel of experts, to field the listeners' questions.

Optional follow-up: Writing
I have left open the topic for this task, but if you want to make it more like IELTS Writing Task 2, you could compose an essay-type title yourself.

Evaluating your performance in this unit on page 122 guides students to reflect on their listening performance. Ask your students to say what other questions/statements could have been included in the list.

Final Review: Ways of continuing to improve your listening

This shorter final session (60–90 minutes) is intended as a summary and reprise, focusing on practical advice for improving listening after the course.

PRE-LISTENING

Pre-listening discussion: Content

1 My answer: Informational and Critical.
2 Judgement of usefulness is, intentionally, an open question. From a listening point of view, programmes likely to be most difficult are cartoons and films, because of their colloquial speech, poor sound quality and background music. The factual programmes are probably easiest to follow, but familiarity with content plays a big part; so one might expect international news to be simpler for students to understand than local news. The accessibility of quiz shows depends on their content, which is of course linked with cultural assumptions and background knowledge. Comedy is in the ear of the listener! American comedy (for example) contains local sociocultural references that may be lost on outsiders, including native listeners from outside the USA.

Reading

This is meant to be done quickly. Once the students have underlined the main point in each suggestion, move straight on to the Listening and note-taking task.

LISTENING

Listening and note-taking

My talk should be fairly straightforward, after the more complex listening the class has been practising in the course. Sample notes are on page 172.

The talk is intended to act as a springboard to the students' discussion in the **Responding** and **Final evaluation** tasks.

AFTER LISTENING

Responding

Of course, the ten suggestions came from individuals studying in an ESL context. If you are teaching in an EFL setting, ask your students to think of ways of adapting the suggestions. As you will see, the ten students' suggestions are quite varied and include ones that I personally would not have thought of. It's important to stress that these strategies worked for the people who are recommending them. They are options to be tried out, not models.

I hope the students (and you) will find the final discussion enlightening and stimulating. I find that listening to students reporting their first-hand experiences of language learning is a fruitful source of insight for my classroom teaching, as well as for students' independent learning.

Listening on the Net

For a comprehensive listing of listening websites that you and your class could follow up, see Section IV of Rost (2002) and Andy Gillett's EAP website http://www.uefap.co.uk/

Appendix: Vocabulary in academic listening

The Academic Word List

A student's knowledge of L2 vocabulary obviously influences how well they understand texts in that language. Research has been done on how large a learner's recognition vocabulary needs to be for them to read effectively. There is general agreement that the 2,000 most frequently used words of English account for about 75 per cent of the lexis in general reading.

In the case of learners of English reading texts for academic purposes, the question to ask is: what is needed in addition to that basic foundation? In a study devoted to this key question, Averill Coxhead of the University of Wellington has developed the *Academic Word List* (Coxhead 2000). This word list comprises the 570 keywords (word families) occurring most frequently in a 3.5 million-word corpus of academic English from four broad groupings, namely the Arts, Science, Law and Commerce.

The *Academic Word List* (AWL) is available at http://www.uvw.ac.nz/lals/divl/awl

Coxhead found that, between them, the first 1,000 most frequent words, the second 1,000 most frequent words and the 570 *AWL* keywords provided more than 85 per cent coverage of the academic texts she analysed. The respective percentages for the three categories were approximately 70, 5 and 10. So to read effectively in their academic subject in English, it is likely that an international student will need to know at least the most frequent 2,000 words and the *AWL* keywords.

So far, most vocabulary research has focused on the written word. When it comes to listening to academic lectures, however, a student also needs to know how a word sounds when used in natural speech by speakers with a range of accents. For students more used to reading English – seeing the words as defined shapes on paper or screen – than to hearing it, this can be a major problem. However, spoken English does offer some compensation: to counterbalance listeners' extra difficulty in recognising words as they are being uttered, speech typically features a higher proportion of the commonest vocabulary. This is reflected in the figures for the vocabulary in the ten recordings used in this book.

Table 1: Relative frequency of vocabulary in Study Listening lectures

	minutes (approx)	words	percentage			
			1st 1000	2nd 1000	AWL	off-list
Introduction	3	417	87	3	7	3
1 Urbanisation	6	850	86	3	7	4
2 Academic cultures	7	1008	86	3	5	6
3 Teleworking	10	1554	85	4	5	6
4 Language strategies	11	1678	82	6	5	7
5 Preventive medicine	12	1748	76	7	4	13
6 Cloning	14	2021	70	5	6	19
7 Quality of life	14	1456	80	4	10	6
8 Climate change	23	2874	80	5	7	8
Final review	6	872	88	4	3	5

Notes:
1 The *words* figure is a total of all the words shown in the transcript, including hesitations noises *um* and *uh*.
2 *Off-list* words are those not occurring in the previous three columns.

The table suggests that – from the lexical point of view – students will find Harry Griffin's lecture on cloning the most demanding in the book. For this reason I have included more *Pre-listening: Language* work in Unit 6 than for the others, and have made suggestions in the *Teaching notes* for ways of compensating for the higher load of (probably) unfamiliar lexis.

In case you would like to focus – before or after the students listen – on the *AWL* keywords the speakers used in the ten recordings, here they are in alphabetical order by lecture.

Introduction

academic areas aspect brief crucial focus functions lecture lecturer links mental obviously research route series source technical topics vocabulary whereas

1 Problems of urbanisation

adequately adults affected area assistance consequences consequently constitutes create distribution dramatic economic economy financial infrastructure instance labour migrate migration motivated obviously policy process promote research resolve stresses tradition traffic urban

2 Differences between academic cultures

academic analyse assumptions authors aware communicate conclusion constituted contrast culture data defined defining definition evidence focus grade hence logically method outcome overseas posed primary procedures project reliable research researchers sections similar sources style task text variables

3 Teleworking and distance learning

adequately affects aids alternatives areas assistants available benefits briefly communicate computer consumption contact conventional converted converting corresponding domestic economic eliminates equip equipment expert exploited facilities finally flexibility granted implications individuals involved involves issue job link major motivated motivation normal obtain obvious occupations parallel principal professionals requires research role scheduled schedules sector specifically stress stressful sum surveys technical technological traffic vital

4 Language strategies for awkward situations

academic adjustment adult ambiguity approach area automatically category challenged circumstances communication conflict contexts conventional defined definition domain economy eventually excluded exclusion formulae functions image imply imprecise interactions issues maintain media mental military minimise negative orientation period physical positive psychologists range research resources response sex sexual significance sociologists sophisticated straightforward strategy substituted summed team thereby utterance vague vagueness verbal

5 Targets for preventive medicine

affected areas available civil components conclusion consequences contrast contributing create detect devices distributing diverse eliminate environment external factors finally goals incidence individual involved involves labour legal major medical mental minority obvious odd period practitioner research resources revolution role similarities strategy survived target task

6 Cloning: The significance of Dolly

approach appropriate area availability benefits briefly capable community considerable converts couples create cultured debate demonstrated differentiated differentiation ethical evidence functioning inappropriately insert inserting insight institute intervening involved irreversible links manipulations matured mechanisms media modifications modify motivation normal nuclear occur overall per cent persist positive potentially precision presumed previously procedure process project proportion prospective range reconstruct reconstructed regulated rejection reliable removed requirements research sequence species specific specifically speculation technique technology theory transfer transferred ultimately

7 Measuring quality of life

achieve adult affecting aggregate analysed annual area aspects assuming attainment availability briefly commented commissioned components concentrating concept conclusion consequences consume consumption context contributor cultural cultures data definition dimension domain domestic economic economics economist element encountered environment exclusion factors final financial goals identified illustrated impact income index indicates indicator individual irrational issue issues links major maximum medical mental methodology minimum normally objective obtain obviously perceive perception physical primary proportion psychologists published ratio reliable research researchers restricted security similar status subjective summarised summary themes traditionally traditions transparent valid vast vision

8 Climate change: Evidence and actions

accurately achieve adapt adequately affect apparent areas authoritative availability bias biased challenge channel comments complex computer concentration confirm conflicting consensus consequences consumption core coupling cycle cycling data debate diverse domestic economic economy energy environment environmental evidence experts extract factored factors final fund generating generation global impact imposed individual infrastructure inherently instance intensive interactions issue legally linked major media occur output panel perceived period phenomenon predict previous primarily processes prospect protocol radical range reconstruct refined regions reinforcing required requires research responsive restructuring revolution security series significant simulate simultaneously stability status suspended target terrorist traces transport trends tropical ultimately urban utilities variability variable varied vehicles whereas widespread

Final review: Ways of continuing to improve your listening

accurate approximations automatic expand exposure lecture lecturer linked location obviously processing quote research similar spontaneously stressed structure variation version vocabulary

VocabProfile software

The software I used to produce the data for the vocabulary table is *VocabProfile*. It was originally developed by Paul Nation and Batia Laufer, and is available on the *Compleat Lexical Tutor* website developed by Tom Cobb on http://132.208.224.131/

Once you have logged in to the *VocabProfile* website, you simply paste in the text you want to analyse. *VocabProfile* produces an analysis showing your text with each word highlighted in a colour showing which of the various frequency lists (first 1000, second 1000, *AWL* or off-list) they belong to. It also prints out alphabetical compilations for each category, like those I have used for *Study Listening*.

The 'off-list' category in *VocabProfile* covers a range of word types, including slang, proper nouns and narrow specialist terms, which means that not all the words appearing 'off-list' will be unknown to your students.

In the case of the lecture on Cloning (Unit 6), I would break down the 93 'off-list' words into the following five categories.

General vocabulary
activated announcement biologist competent compromised delete developmental endangered ending extinct fanciful fascination fiction fragmented fused fusion hopelessly imaginatively ingenuity lifespan maternal mobilised mooted museum obesity oversized patients pragmatic pregnant proposition realms reawakened resort resurrect seminal shortfall specialised spectacular versatile viable

Technical vocabulary
blastocyst cell clone cloning DNA embryo enucleated fertilisation foetal foetus gene genome gestation gland immune implant infertile mammal mammary manipulators marsupial microscope nucleus offspring Parkinson's disease pipettes placenta protein pulse replicating reprogrammed sperm surrogate transgenic xenotransplantation

Colloquial vocabulary
fake hopefully tremendous vibes

Proper nouns
Australia Hawaii Japan Jurassic Park New Zealand Roslin Institute

Animals
kitten panda Tasmanian tiger

VocabProfile is a really excellent learning and teaching tool, and is only one of many useful programs on the *Compleat Lexical Tutor* site.

References

Anderson, K. and Lynch, T. (1996) *PROFILE – Principles, Resources and Options for the Independent Learner of English*. Edinburgh: Institute for Applied Language Studies, University of Edinburgh.

Ballard, B. (1984) Improving student writing: an integrated approach to cultural adjustment. In R. Williams, J. Swales and J. Kirkman (eds) *Common Ground: Shared Interests in ESP and Communication Skills*. ELT Documents 117, London: British Council.

Coleman, H. (1991) The testing of 'appropriate behaviour' in an academic context. In P. Adams, B. Heaton and P. Howarth (eds) *Socio-Cultural Issues in English for Academic Purposes*. Modern English Publications/British Council.

Coxhead, A. (2000) A new academic word list. *TESOL Quarterly*, 34/2: 213–238.

Dudley-Evans, A. and Johns, T. (1981) A team-teaching approach to lecture comprehension for overseas students. In *The Teaching of Listening Comprehension*. ELT Documents Special. London: British Council.

Field, J. (1998) The changing face of listening. *English Teaching Professional*, 6: 12–14.

Hamp-Lyons, L. and Heasley, B. (2004) *Study Writing*. Cambridge: Cambridge University Press.

Jin, L. and Cortazzi, M. (1996) 'This way is very different from Chinese ways'; EAP needs and academic culture. In M. Hewings and T. Dudley-Evans (eds) *Evaluation and Course Design in EAP*. Basingstoke: Prentice Hall Macmillan.

Lynch, T. (1996) *Communication in the Language Classroom*. Oxford: Oxford University Press.

Ridgway, T. (2000) Listening strategies – I beg your pardon? *ELT Journal*, 54/2: 179–85.

Rost, M. (2002) *Teaching and Researching Listening*. Harlow: Longman.

Rubin, J. and Thompson, I. (1982) *How to Be a Successful Language Learner*. Boston: Heinle and Heinle.

Schumacher, E.F. (1973) *Small is Beautiful: a Study of Economics as if People Mattered*. London: Sphere Books.

Tauroza, S. (1995) Trouble-shooting. In D. Nunan and L. Miller (eds) *New Ways in Teaching Listening*. Alexandria, VA: TESOL.

Vandergrift, L. (1999) Facilitating second language listening comprehension: acquiring successful listening strategies. *ELT Journal*, 53/3: 168–76.

White, G. (1998) *Listening*. Oxford: Oxford University Press.